THE **WOK** COOKBOOK

THE **WOK** COOKBOOK

BY GINA STEER

APPLE

A QUINTET BOOK

Published by Apple Press
6 Blundell Street
London N7 9BH

ISBN 1-84092-312-1

This book was conceived, designed and produced by
Quintet Publishing Limited
6 Blundell Street
London N7 9BH

Senior Project Editor: Toria Leitch
Editor: Anna Bennett
Designer: Deep Creative
Photographer: Ian Garlick
Food Stylist: Kathryn Hawkins
Creative Director: Richard Dewing

Typeset in Great Britain by Central Southern Typesetters, Eastbourne
Manufactured in Hong Kong by Regent Publishing Services Limited
Printed in China by Leefung-Asco Printers Trading Limited

ACKNOWLEDGEMENTS

I would like to thank Juliet Barker for all her hard word in helping me test these recipes and of course I cannot forget my family who as ever have eaten every one of these dishes, commenting throughout. Also the photographer, Ian Garlick and the food stylist, Kathryn Hawkins, who have done such a great visual job.

CONTENTS

INTRODUCTION

Welcome to the world of wok cooking. Once you try it you will be instantly converted. It has to be one of the fastest ways of cooking, which is good news with today's frantic lifestyle.

Wok cuisine originated in Asia, but once introduced to the West, caught on quickly as cooks realized its vast potential. This was also helped by the popularity of Chinese food in many countries. Consumers were so impressed with the vast array of delicious and colourful dishes offered by this cuisine that they wanted to be able to reproduce these dishes for themselves at home.

The shape of the wok ensures that the heat is evenly distributed over the base of the pan. Because of this concave shape, the whole wok becomes a cooking surface. The food can be moved about inside the wok, which enables it to cook rapidly, preserving all of the valuable nutrients. It is a very healthy way of cooking because usually only a minimum amount of oil is used.

A wide range of ingredients can be cooked in a wok, and it is extremely easy to adapt Western recipes to wok cooking. The current trend towards a fusion of Eastern and Western cuisines is providing a host of recipes that are new, exciting and suitable for all tastes and cultures. I guarantee you will find this book a valuable addition to your kitchen library.

CHOOSING AND SEASONING YOUR WOK

When choosing your wok, choose one that is large enough – 36 cm/14 in in diameter is a good size. Look for one with deep sides. A heavier wok, made from carbon steel, is better than one made from light stainless steel or aluminium because the lighter ones tend to scorch. It is possible to buy electric woks with their own element, but these tend not to heat up to a sufficiently high temperature.

It is also important to choose the correct wok for your cooker. If you have an electric stove, you will need to buy a wok with a flat bottom so that the heat can be conducted through its base. A round-bottomed wok can only be used on a gas stove.

If you buy a wok with a non-stick surface you do not need to season the wok: simply wash in warm soapy water, dry thoroughly and wipe with a little oil.

After use, cool slightly and fill with warm soapy water. Leave for a few minutes, then wipe with a sponge or cloth. Do not use a scouring powder or pad. Clean the outside of the wok regularly. Scouring pads can be used on the outside if necessary. Some non-stick woks can be put in the dishwasher but this will affect the appearance of the wok; the surface will become dull and discoloured.

It is now possible to buy non-stick woks with a thermospot heat indicator. This has a red indicator in the centre of the base of the wok that changes colour when heating, indicating that the wok is at the correct temperature for the oil to be added for cooking to commence.

If you buy a traditional wok you will need to season it before use. First, rinse well and scrub with a cream cleanser and water to remove the machine oil, then place on the stove over low heat. Pour in 3 tablespoons of oil. Rub this oil all over the inside of the wok with paper towels and heat on the burner for 10 to 15 minutes until really hot. Wipe with paper towels: you will find the paper will be black. Repeat this heating and wiping until the paper is clean. The wok is now ready for use. It will become darker and even more seasoned with use.

Once seasoned the wok should not be washed with detergent because this will destroy the non-stick surface. After cooking, rinse the wok under hot running water, scrub with a brush, then return to the heat to dry off. Once dry, smear with a little oil before storing.

OTHER EQUIPMENT

You will also need a few other pieces of equipment to ensure that your wok cooking is a success.

• **Wok Stand** This is a metal ring or frame that is used to keep the wok steady on the burner. It is especially useful if you want to use your wok for steaming, deep-frying or braising.

• **Wok Lid** A dome-like cover used for steaming. It may come with the wok or can be purchased separately. You can use foil instead, but make sure it fits snugly.

• **Spatula** The best type to use is a long-handled spatula rather like a small shovel, for scooping and stirring the food in the wok.

• **Rack** If you use the wok as a steamer, a wooden or metal rack is required to stand above the water level and support the plate of food to be steamed.

• **Bamboo brush** A bundle of stiff, split bamboo used for cleaning the wok without scrubbing off the seasoned surface. A soft washing-up brush would also do the job.

• **Cleavers** Food is often finely shredded in Asian cuisine. A cleaver performs this job brilliantly and can also chop up bones, herbs, vegetables and a host of other ingredients. There are three different types: a lightweight one with a narrow blade for delicate foods; a medium weight for general cutting, chopping and crushing; and a heavy-duty cleaver for chopping bones. Choose a good-quality cleaver and keep it well sharpened.

• **Steamers** Bamboo steamers come in a variety of sizes. To use, fill with the food to be steamed, then place on a rack in the wok, with water underneath. Clean damp cheesecloth or waxed paper can be placed over the slats on the base where the food to be cooked is placed. This prevents the food from falling through. A tight-fitting lid is placed on top. If necessary, several steamers can be placed on top of each other.

TECHNIQUES

With wok cooking it is important that a few cutting and cooking techniques are followed to ensure a good result every time.

• **Meat** should always be sliced across the grain in order to break up the fibres and make it more tender after cooking.

• **Vegetables** are better if sliced diagonally. This exposes more of the surface of the vegetable, which cooks it more quickly. To do this, angle the knife or cleaver at a slant and cut.

• **Scoring** Some foods, such as whole fish or pieces of poultry, are often scored. This means piercing the surface of the food to help the heat to penetrate more quickly and give a more attractive finish at the end of the cooking time. With a cleaver or sharp knife, make cuts at an angle across the food, taking care not to cut right through.

• **Blanching** This is covering foods with boiling water or moderately hot oil and leaving for a few minutes before draining. This softens the food so it takes less time at the final cooking. Meat is often blanched to remove any scum, thus giving a more attractive appearance and a better taste. Vegetables such as carrots or broccoli are blanched in boiling water then plunged into cold water – this reduces the final cooking time and preserves their bright colour.

• **Stir-frying** Before you start to cook, it is important to have all your ingredients already prepared. Heat the wok before adding the oil (this is very important as it ensures that the food does not stick to the wok and ensures an even distribution of heat). Add the oil and heat it until it is almost smoking, unless you intend to flavour the oil. If flavouring the oil, heat the wok then add the oil and heat (but not to smoking) then add the flavouring ingredients such as chilli, shallots, ginger and lemon grass. Toss them in the oil. Then, depending on the recipe, either remove the flavouring ingredients or add the next ingredients.

• **Movement** Keep the food moving in the wok so that it cooks evenly.

• **Thickening** When thickening a dish with cornflour at the end of cooking, draw the wok off the heat and stir in the blended cornflour, stir, then return to the heat and cook stirring until thickened.

• **Draining** Any food to be deep-fried should be drained thoroughly on paper towels before cooking. If the food has been marinated, remove it with a slotted draining spoon from the marinade and allow any excess marinade to drip back into the bowl. Drain the food again after cooking on paper towels.

• **Steaming** If you are using a bamboo steamer, pour about 5 cm/2 in of water into the wok and bring to the simmering point. Place the food in the steamer, and set the steamer in the wok where it can sit safely wedged or perched on the sloping sides. Cover the steamer with its lid and steam. Add more water as necessary.

INGREDIENTS

- **Oil** The best types of oil for woking are groundnut or vegetable oil because they can be heated to a high temperature without burning. Do not use olive oil. Normally sesame oil is added at the end of the cooking time to add flavour and a burst of heat.
- **Flavourings** A wide variety of ingredients are used to flavour the food – garlic, ginger, galangal, (similar to ginger but with a milder citrus-pine flavour), chillies, lemon grass (which has a distinct citrus flavour), kaffir lime leaves (also with a citrus-pine flavour), fresh chopped coriander, basil and sesame seeds. There are also several sauces:
- **Hot chilli sauce** A bright red sauce, made from chillies, sugar, salt and vinegar. It is sometimes used in cooking, more often as a dipping sauce. There is also a sweet chilli sauce which contains more sugar and is used mainly as a dipping sauce.
- **Hoisin sauce** A thick dark brown, sweet and spicy sauce made from soybeans, vinegar, sugar and spices.
- **Oyster sauce** A thick, brown sauce made from oysters that have been cooked in soy sauce. Used as a condiment as well as in cooking.
- **Chilli bean sauce** Made from soybeans and chillies; very hot and spicy.
- **Yellow bean sauce** A thick, spicy, aromatic sauce made from yellow beans, flour and salt, fermented together. There is also black bean sauce, made from black beans. Both are used to flavour dishes and are added during cooking.
- **Soy sauce** Both light and dark versions are used extensively in Asian cuisine as a flavouring and condiment. They are made from soya beans that have been fermented.
- **Fish sauce (*nam pla*)** Made from fermented fish, this is used in Thai foods as a seasoning. As the name implies, it has a strong fish taste.
- **Plum sauce** Made from Chinese plums which have been simmered with fresh ginger and chilli, giving a sweet chilli-flavoured sauce with overtones of sweetness from the plums. It can be used as a dipping sauce or added to stir-fries to give a fruit and spice flavour.

- **Rice vinegar** is popular in Asian cuisine and made from rice. It can vary from spicy and tart to sweet and pungent. There are white rice vinegars, black rice vinegars and red rice vinegars. They can be substituted with cider or white wine vinegar.
- **Rice wine**, also known as sake, made from fermented rice. A commonly used ingredient for dressings, sauces and marinades. It can be substituted with dry sherry.
- **Rice** and **noodles** provide the main bulk in an Asian meal. Choose from long-grain, basmati, Thai fragrant (jasmine) rice, which becomes soft and sticky on cooking or glutinous rice, which is also known as sweet, sticky or waxy rice (types available include Japanese, Chinese and Thai). Normally Thai rice is served with Thai-style dishes, long-grain rice with Chinese and Indonesian dishes and basmati is served with Indian foods.
- **Noodles** are very versatile and vary considerably. Dried noodles are usually soaked in water for up to 20 minutes, depending on the variety. Once softened the cooking time is brief. The noodles will double in bulk after soaking.
- **Mung bean noodles** are also known as bean thread or cellophane noodles; after soaking they acquire a jelly-like texture.
- **Stir-fry** or **rice stick noodles** or **rice vermicelli** are thin, brittle and semi-translucent. They can either be soaked or, if to be served crisp, fried without soaking.
- **Soba noodles** are made from buckwheat flour and are boiled before use in noodle dishes or salads.
- **Udon noodles** are thick Japanese wheat noodles normally eaten with a soy-based broth.
- **Egg noodles**, which are wheat-based, come either as slender or medium noodles and are the most widely available ones in the Western world. They can be bought both fresh and dried, and can be boiled in water as for pasta, then tossed into the wok. They are either served plain or tossed with soy sauce and flavourings.

SAUCES AND PASTES

Dipping sauces and pastes are very important in Asian cuisine and can be bought or simply made at home. Try the following sauces for yourself which are some of my favourites and then when you get more adventurous, devise a few of your own.

- **Red Chilli Paste** Seed 3 to 4 red hot chillies and steam over a pan of simmering water for 15 minutes. Then place in a blender with 1 chopped onion, 3 crushed garlic cloves, 2 teaspoons ground coriander, 1 tablespoon grated root ginger, the grated zest and juice of 2 limes, seasoning to taste and 3 tablespoons oil. Blend to a thick paste, adding extra oil as required. Store in a screw-top jar in the refrigerator and use within 1 week.
- **Green Chilli Paste.** Seed 3 to 4 green jalapeño chillies and place in a blender with 3 crushed garlic cloves, the chopped inside of 3 lemon grass stalks, 6 trimmed and chopped spring onions and 2 to 3 kaffir lime leaves. Blend with 1 teaspoon honey and 2 to 3 tablespoons lime juice, then stir in 2 tablespoons chopped fresh coriander. Store in a screw-top jar in the refrigerator for up to 1 week.
- **Ginger and Spring Onion Sauce** Heat the wok, add 3 tablespoons oil, and heat to almost smoking. Stir in 4 trimmed and chopped spring onions, 2 teaspoons ground ginger and 1 tablespoon light soy sauce. Once it sizzles it is ready for use.
- **Sweet-and-Sour Sauce** Blend together 3 tablespoons dark soy sauce and honey with 1 finely chopped garlic clove, 1 tablespoon rice wine, 2 teaspoons chilli sauce and a generous pinch of Chinese five-spice powder. Use as required.

When you cook an Asian meal, select just two or three dishes and serve them with some plain boiled rice or noodles. Choose dishes that harmonize in colour and texture. If you like you can divide the dishes into Western-style courses, serving them as simple one-dish meals, appetizers or hors d'oeuvres.

Before you start, read the recipe all the way through so that you are clear about the different stages. Then prepare yourself for a real taste explosion as you feast on the fabulous flavours from the East.

APPETIZERS AND
HORS D'OEUVRES

SESAME PRAWN BALLS

THESE MAKE A DELICIOUS HORS D'OEUVRE OR APPETIZER; THEY CAN BE
PREPARED AHEAD OF TIME AND COOKED JUST BEFORE THEY ARE REQUIRED.

Makes **12 to 14**

Preparation time **15 minutes plus 1 hour**
  chilling time

Cooking time **6 to 9 minutes**

450 g/1 lb peeled prawns, defrosted if frozen
4 spring onions, trimmed and chopped
5 cm/2 in piece root ginger, peeled and grated
1 red jalapeño chilli, seeded and chopped
2 Tbsp chopped fresh parsley
25 g/1 oz fresh white breadcrumbs
Salt and freshly ground black pepper
4 Tbsp sesame seeds
Groundnut oil for frying

TO GARNISH
Chopped chilli and lime wedges

Dry the prawns in paper towels, squeezing out any excess moisture, and place in a food processor with the spring onions, root ginger, chilli, parsley, breadcrumbs and seasoning. Blend in short sharp bursts until the ingredients are fine chopped and blended. Chill for 30 minutes.

Place the sesame seeds in a shallow bowl. Shape the prawn mixture into apricot-sized balls and roll them in the sesame seeds. Place on a plate, cover lightly and chill in the refrigerator for at least 30 minutes.

Heat the wok, half-fill with the oil and heat to 190°C/375°F. Cook the prawn balls a few at a time for 2 to 3 minutes, or until golden and crisp. Remove from the wok with a slotted draining spoon and drain on paper towels.

Repeat until all the balls have been cooked. Serve warm, garnished with chopped chilli and lime wedges.

SESAME PRAWN TOASTS

THESE CAN BE PREPARED AHEAD OF TIME AND COOKED
JUST BEFORE THEY ARE REQUIRED.

Serves **6 to 8**
Preparation time **5 minutes**
Cooking time **10 to 12 minutes**

350 g/12 oz peeled prawns, defrosted if frozen
1 medium egg
4 spring onions, trimmed and finely chopped
1 to 2 bird's eye red chillies, seeded and finely chopped
Freshly milled salt to taste
1 Tbsp light soy sauce
8 thin slices day-old bread
3 Tbsp sesame seeds
About 300 ml/½ pt oil for deep-frying

Dry the peeled prawns thoroughly on paper towels and place in a food processor with the egg, spring onions, chillies, salt and soy sauce. Blend in short sharp bursts to form a rough paste.

Spread the paste onto the pieces of bread to a depth of 1.25 cm/½ in and cut into small oblongs about 2.5 cm/1 in wide and 7.5 cm/3 in long. Sprinkle with the sesame seeds.

Heat the oil in the wok to 190°C/375°F and fry the sesame toasts, paste-side down, for 2 minutes, or until crisp and golden. Drain on paper towels and serve immediately.

STEAMED SCALLOPS WITH
SPINACH AND RICE NOODLES

CHOOSE PLUMP, WHITE SCALLOPS, AVOIDING THOSE THAT LOOK TIRED AND GREY.
IF BUYING FRESH AND NOT USING IMMEDIATELY, FREEZE ON THE DAY OF PURCHASE.

Soak the rice noodles in boiling water for about 4 minutes or until soft. Drain thoroughly and set aside.

Clean the scallops and place on a sheet of non-stick baking paper in the top of a bamboo steamer. Blend two of the crushed garlic cloves with the lime juice, zest and soy sauce, and sprinkle over the scallops. Place the steamer over a wok or a large pan filled with boiling water and steam for 6 to 8 minutes, or until the scallops become opaque. Take care not to overcook or the scallops will be tough.

Meanwhile, heat the wok and add the groundnut oil. When hot, stir-fry the remaining garlic and spring onions for 2 minutes. Add the spinach and stir-fry for 2 minutes, or until wilted.

Add the noodles, fish sauce and sesame oil. Stir-fry for 1 minute, or until heated through. Arrange on individual serving plates, top with the scallops, and sprinkle with the chopped coriander before serving.

Serves **4**
Preparation time **10 minutes plus**
  4 minutes soaking time
Cooking time **6 to 8 minutes**

175 g/6 oz stir-fry rice noodles
12 fresh scallops
4 garlic cloves, peeled and crushed
2 Tbsp lime juice
1 Tbsp grated lime zest
2 Tbsp light soy sauce
1 Tbsp groundnut oil
6 spring onions, trimmed and
  chopped
100 g/4 oz spinach, tough leaves and
  stalks discarded
1 Tbsp Thai fish sauce (nam pla)
1 tsp sesame oil
1 Tbsp chopped fresh coriander

CHICKEN AND SWEETCORN SOUP

USE FRESH CORN ON THE COB IF POSSIBLE. THE KERNELS ARE FAR SWEETER AND CRISPER THAN FROZEN OR CANNED AND GIVE A WONDERFUL CRISP TEXTURE TO THE SOUP.

Rinse the corn cobs and discard the silky threads if necessary. Fill the wok with boiling water and add the corn cobs. Simmer gently for 15 minutes or until tender. Drain and cool before stripping off the kernels from the cobs. Set aside.

Cut the chicken into very fine shreds. Heat 150 ml/¼ pt of the chicken stock and gently poach the chicken shreds with the dried chillies for 2 minutes, or until opaque.

Add the remaining stock, the corn kernels, soy sauce, spring onions and sesame oil and simmer in the wok for 2 minutes.

Blend the cornflour with 2 tablespoons water. Stir into the wok and cook, stirring, until the soup has thickened slightly, and serve.

Serves **4 to 6**
Preparation time **15 minutes plus cooling time**
Cooking time **20 minutes**

2 ears of corn on the cob, husks removed if fresh
225 g/8 oz boneless, skinless chicken breasts
900 ml/1½ pt chicken stock
½ to 1 tsp dried crushed chillies
2 to 3 Tbsp dark soy sauce
6 spring onions, trimmed and chopped
1 tsp sesame oil
4 Tsp cornflour

COCONUT AND GINGER SALMON LAKSA

THIS DELICIOUS SOUP IS INSPIRED BY THE PACIFIC RIM TREND, A STYLE OF COOKING THAT COMBINES
THE BEST OF EASTERN AND WESTERN CUISINES TO PROVIDE NEW AND INNOVATIVE DISHES.

Place the egg noodles in a large bowl, cover with boiling water
and leave for 3 minutes. Drain the noodles and set aside.

Heat the wok and add the oil. When hot gently stir-fry the garlic,
ginger, chillies and leeks for 2 minutes. Add the saffron strands,
stir once, then add the salmon and stir-fry for 1 minute.

Pour in the coconut milk and stock. Bring to the boil and
simmer gently for 2 minutes. Add the reserved noodles and the
soy sauce. Return to the boil and simmer gently for 3 to 4
minutes. Blend the cornflour with 1 tablespoon water, add to the
pan and cook for 1 minute until thickened. Sprinkle with the
spring onions and serve immediately.

Serves **4**
Preparation time **10 minutes**
Cooking time **10 minutes**

75 g/3 oz fine egg noodles
1 Tbsp vegetable or sunflower oil
3 garlic cloves, peeled
and crushed
5 cm/2 in piece root ginger,
peeled and grated
1 to 2 bird's eye chillies, seeded
and sliced

2 baby leeks, trimmed and sliced
A few saffron strands
225 g/8 oz salmon fillet, skinned
and diced
300 ml/½ pt coconut milk
450 ml/¾ pt fish stock
2 Tbsp light soy sauce
1 Tbsp cornflour
3 spring onions, trimmed and
diagonally sliced (optional)

CRAB SPRING ROLLS

THE FILLING FOR THESE DELICIOUS ROLLS CAN CONSIST OF CHICKEN, PORK, PRAWNS
OR VEGETABLES. THEY ARE CERTAINLY WELL WORTH THE EFFORT IN MAKING.

Remove the membranes and seeds from the red pepper and finely
shred. Set aside.

Heat the wok and add the sesame oil. Stir-fry the red pepper, Parma
ham, chilli, lime zest, spring onions and carrots for 1 to 2 minutes, or
until just starting to soften. Remove and place in a bowl together with
the crab meat, bean sprouts, soy sauce and cayenne pepper. Mix well
and place in a sieve or colander to drain.

Blend the flour with 2 to 3 tablespoons water to form a paste
and set aside.

Place a spring roll wrapper on a work counter and place 2 to
3 tablespoons of the filling onto the wrapper. Brush the edges with
a little of the flour paste and turn into the centre. Roll up to form
a cigar shape and seal the edge. Press firmly together to seal well.
Repeat with the remaining wrappers and filling. (If using phyllo
pastry, fold a sheet of pastry in half and then in half again, brushing
the pastry with a little water before folding over. Proceed as for the
spring roll wrappers, but remember that phyllo pastry dries out
quickly, so keep it wrapped when not in use.)

Heat the wok, add the oil to a depth of about 10 cm/4 in, and
heat to 190°C/375°F. Deep-fry about 3 to 4 spring rolls for about
3 minutes, turning them over as they fry, until golden and crisp.
Drain on paper towels and repeat until they are all cooked.
Serve warm, garnished with lime wedges.

Makes **12**
Preparation time **20 minutes**
Cooking time **12 to 14 minutes**

1 small red pepper

1 Tbsp sesame oil

100 g/4 oz Parma ham, shredded

**1 small green jalapeño chilli,
seeded and finely shredded**

1 Tbsp grated lime zest

**4 spring onions, trimmed and
finely shredded**

100 g/4 oz carrots, peeled and grated

**200 g/7 oz fresh or canned white
crabmeat, drained if necessary**

75 g/3 oz bean sprouts

1 Tbsp light soy sauce

Pinch of cayenne pepper or to taste

4 Tbsp plain white flour

**1 packet (12 to 16) spring roll
wrappers (or 12 to 14 sheets
phyllo pastry)**

**Vegetable or sunflower oil for
deep-frying**

TO GARNISH
Lime wedges

HOT AND SOUR SOUP

TRY EATING THIS SOUP WHEN YOU ARE FEELING SLIGHTLY UNDER THE WEATHER OR HAVE THE BEGINNINGS OF A COLD. THE CHILLIES IN THE SOUP HELP CLEAR THE SINUSES AND MAKE YOU FEEL BETTER.

Serves **6**

Preparation time **10 minutes plus 20 minutes soaking time**

Cooking time **7 minutes**

15 g/¹/₂ oz dried mushrooms

50 g/2 oz boneless, skinless chicken breast fillets

175 g/6 oz tofu (bean curd), drained

300 ml/1¹/₂ pt chicken stock, preferably home-made

1 to 2 bird's eye chillies, seeded and chopped

3 lemon grass stalks, bruised, outer leaves discarded

1 medium carrot, peeled and cut into thin strips

2 celery stalks, trimmed and cut into thin strips

2 to 3 Tbsp dark soy sauce

75 g/3 oz mangetout, halved

100 g/4 oz bean sprouts

2 Tbsp cornflour

2 Tbsp dry sherry

2 Tbsp chopped fresh coriander

Soak the mushrooms in 150 ml/¹/₄ pt almost-boiling water for 20 minutes. Drain, setting aside the mushrooms and soaking liquid. Chop the rehydrated mushrooms into small pieces if necessary. Cut the chicken into thin strips and the tofu into small dice. Set aside.

Heat the wok, then add the stock with the chillies and lemon grass, and simmer for 3 minutes. Add the mushrooms, soaking liquid, chicken strips, tofu, carrot, celery and soy sauce. Bring to the boil, and simmer for 2 minutes. Skim if necessary and add the mangetout and bean sprouts. Cook for another minute.

Blend the cornflour with the sherry, stir into the wok and cook, stirring until slightly thickened. Stir in the coriander, heat for 30 seconds and serve.

MISO FISH SOUP

MISO SOUP IS A TRADITIONAL JAPANESE SOUP. MISO IS MADE FROM AGED AND FERMENTED SOYA BEANS.

Serves **4**

Preparation time **10 minutes**

Cooking time **8 to 10 minutes**

1.2 l/2 pts fish or vegetable stock

1.25 cm/¹/₂ in piece root ginger, peeled and shredded

1 tsp mirin

1 large carrot, peeled and cut into ribbons

1 courgette, trimmed and cut into ribbons

1 red serrano chilli, seeded and chopped

225 g/8 oz firm white fish fillets

100 g/4 oz fresh salmon fillet

100 g/4 oz raw tiger prawns, peeled

3 Tbsp miso paste

1 to 2 Tbsp soy sauce

TO SERVE

Grated daikon and fried seaweed

Place the stock in the wok with the ginger, mirin, carrots, courgette and chilli, and bring to the boil. Simmer for 6 minutes.

Cut the fish into small pieces and add to the wok together with the raw prawns and miso paste. Continue to simmer for 2 to 3 minutes or until the fish is done.

Add soy sauce to taste and serve in individual bowls, topped with the daikon and seaweed.

SOLE GOUJONS WITH GINGER

THE ROASTED SEASONING IN THIS RECIPE IS USED IN A VARIETY OF THE DISHES IN THIS BOOK, MAKE AND KEEP IN AN AIRTIGHT CONTAINER AND USE AS REQUIRED. THE SEASONING WILL WORK WELL WITH ALL MEAT AND POULTRY AS WELL AS FISH.

Heat a wok until hot but not smoking. Add the salt and peppercorns and stir-fry for 1 to 2 minutes, or until the salt and peppercorns begin to smoke slightly and give off a roasted aroma. Remove from the heat and cool; either grind immediately and store in a screw-top jar or store whole and grind as required.

Pour 2 tablespoons boiling water over the grated ginger and leave for 10 minutes to infuse. Drain and set aside the liquid.

Blend the soured cream or crème fraîche with the reserved ginger liquid, spring onions and chopped coriander. Spoon into a small serving dish, cover and store in the refrigerator until required.

Rinse the sole fillets and cut into 1.25 cm/½ in strips. Mix 1 teaspoon of the roasted salt and pepper mixture with the ginger and cornflour and use to coat the sole fillets.

Heat the wok, add the oil to a depth of 10 cm/4 in and heat to 190°C/375°F.

Deep-fry a few sole strips at a time for 1 to 2 minutes, or until golden and crisp. Drain on paper towels. Repeat until all the strips have been cooked. Serve immediately with the ginger sauce, sprinkled with a little extra roasted seasoning.

Serves **4**
Preparation time **15 minutes plus 10 minutes infusing time**
Cooking time **10 minutes**

FOR THE ROASTED SEASONING
50 g/2 oz sea salt
50 g/2 oz peppercorns

FOR THE SAUCE
5 cm/2 in piece root ginger, peeled and finely grated or minced
5 Tbsp soured cream or half-fat crème fraîche
3 spring onions, trimmed and finely chopped
1 Tbsp chopped fresh coriander

FOR THE FISH
450 g/1 lb sole fillets
1 tsp minced root ginger or ½ tsp ground ginger
2 to 3 Tbsp cornflour
Oil for deep frying

KING PRAWNS
WITH GARLIC AND BRANDY

KEEP THE TAIL SHELL ON WHEN PEELING PRAWNS. IT LOOKS ATTRACTIVE AND
ALSO MAKES THE PRAWNS EASIER TO HOLD WHEN EATING.

Peel the prawns, leaving the tail intact, removing the heads and the
thin black vein that runs down the back. Rinse, pat dry and place in
a shallow dish. Sprinkle with the garlic, shallots, lime zest and
ginger, then add the soy sauce and Tabasco to taste. Turn the
prawns over gently to coat them lightly with the marinade
ingredients. Cover and marinate in the refrigerator for 30 minutes.

When ready to cook, heat the wok and add the oil. When hot,
add the prawns and the marinade ingredients. Stir-fry for 3 to
4 minutes, or until the prawns are done and have turned pink.

Add the brandy to the wok and heat for 30 seconds. Take the wok off
the heat and either set alight and wait for the flames to subside
before serving or serve immediately on a bed of bitter salad leaves.
Garnish with lime zest.

Serves **4 as an appetizer**
Preparation time **10 minutes plus**
30 minutes marinating time
Cooking time **4 to 5 minutes**

16 raw king prawns
6 garlic cloves, peeled and
finely sliced
2 shallots, peeled and cut
into thin wedges
1 Tbsp grated lime zest
2.5 cm/1 in piece root ginger,
peeled and grated
3 Tbsp light soy sauce
A few dashes Tabasco sauce
2 Tbsp sunflower or vegetable oil
3 to 4 Tbsp brandy

TO SERVE
Bitter salad leaves

TO GARNISH
Lime zest

FISH AND SEAFOOD

MONKFISH WITH PAK CHOI

WHEN SOAKING DRIED MUSHROOMS, IT IS IMPORTANT TO LEAVE THEM IN THE WATER FOR AT LEAST 20 MINUTES. WHERE POSSIBLE, USE THE SOAKING LIQUID IN THE FINISHED DISH TO OBTAIN THE MAXIMUM AMOUNT OF FLAVOUR.

Cover the dried mushrooms with almost-boiling water, let stand for 20 minutes and drain, setting aside 2 tablespoons of the soaking liquid.

Trim and wipe the fish and place on a chopping board. Sprinkle with the Chinese five-spice powder and rub in lightly. Place on a plate, cover and allow to marinate in the refrigerator for at least 1 hour.

Cut the fennel and carrot into thin strips. Thinly slice the onion. Cut the shiitake mushrooms in halves or quarters, depending on size. Shred the pak choi.

When ready to cook, remove the fish from the marinade and cut into bite-sized pieces.

Heat the wok. When hot, add the oil and stir-fry the fish for 2 minutes. Remove and set aside.

Add the prepared vegetables, except the pak choi, and then add the reserved rehydrated dried mushrooms. Stir-fry for 2 to 3 minutes.

Blend the cornflour with the mushroom soaking liquid, the soy sauce and rice wine or sherry.

Pour the blended mixture into the wok with the fish and pak choi. Stir-fry for 1 minute or until the fish is done and the bok choy has wilted. Serve immediately with freshly cooked rice and sprinkled with the flaked almonds.

Serves **4**
Preparation time **10 minutes plus 1 hour marinating time**
Cooking time **6 minutes**

15 g/¹⁄₂ oz dried mushrooms
450 g/1 lb monkfish fillet
2 tsp Chinese five-spice powder
1 head fennel, trimmed
1 large carrot, peeled
1 medium red onion, peeled
100 g/4 oz shiitake mushrooms, wiped
200 g/7 oz pak choi heads
1 Tbsp groundnut oil
2 tsp cornflour
2 Tbsp dark soy sauce
1 Tbsp rice wine or dry sherry

TO SERVE
Freshly cooked rice
1 Tbsp roasted flaked almonds

COD WITH WILTED SPINACH

IF SPINACH IS UNAVAILABLE, USE EITHER PAK CHOI OR CHINESE GREENS, THAT WILL
NEED TO BE SHREDDED BEFORE ADDING TO THE WOK AT THE END OF THE COOKING TIME.

Cut the cod into large cubes, place in a shallow dish and scatter the chopped chilli and garlic over the top. Blend the tomato purée with the vinegar, sherry and orange juice, then pour over the fish. Cover lightly and marinate in the refrigerator for at least 30 minutes, turning the fish over occasionally during this time.

Discard any tough outer leaves and stalks from the spinach, wash thoroughly in plenty of cold water and allow to drain well.

When ready to cook, drain the fish, setting aside the marinade. Heat a wok and add 1 tablespoon of the oil. When hot, stir-fry the fish for 2 to 3 minutes, or until done. Add the marinade and stir-fry for 30 seconds. Remove and keep warm.

Wipe the wok and add the remaining oil. Stir-fry the spinach in two batches, if necessary, for 2 to 3 minutes, or until just beginning to wilt. Add the spring onions and orange zest, stir-fry for 30 seconds and spoon onto a warmed serving platter. Arrange the cod on top and serve immediately.

Serves **4**
Preparation time **5 minutes plus
  30 minutes marinating time**
Cooking time **7 to 10 minutes**

675 g/1½ lb cod fillet
**1 red jalapeño chilli, seeded and
  chopped**
2 garlic cloves, peeled and crushed
2 Tbsp tomato purée
1 Tbsp red wine vinegar
2 Tbsp medium-dry sherry
50 ml/2 fl oz orange juice
675 g/1½ lb spinach
2 Tbsp vegetable oil
6 spring onions, trimmed and sliced
2 Tbsp grated orange zest

WARM SEAFOOD WITH
WILD MUSHROOMS

USE AS WIDE A SELECTION OF SEAFOOD AND MUSHROOMS AS POSSIBLE TO GIVE A GOOD ASSORTMENT OF COLOURS AND A GREAT RANGE OF TEXTURES.

Clean the seafood as necessary. For squid, pull the sac and tentacles apart; remove the backbone and entrails from the sac and discard the head. Rinse thoroughly. For the scallops, discard the black vein if necessary and cut in half if large. Cut the monkfish into small pieces. If using fresh prawns, remove the heads and peel. Rinse lightly and dry on paper towels.

Heat the wok, add 1 tablespoon of the oil, and stir-fry the chilli, garlic and shallots for 2 minutes. Add the mushrooms and continue to stir-fry for 3 minutes. Remove from the wok and wipe clean if necessary.

Add the remaining oil to the hot wok and stir-fry the fish for 3 to 4 minutes. Add the mushrooms with the rice wine, soy sauce and basil. Stir-fry for 1 minute or until the fish is done, then serve immediately with warm crusty bread and a tossed green and mixed pepper salad.

Serves **4**
Preparation time **15 minutes**
Cooking time **9 to 10 minutes**

450 g/1 lb fresh mixed seafood, such as squid, scallops, monkfish and large prawns
2 Tbsp groundnut oil
1 red jalapeño chilli, seeded and chopped
2 to 3 garlic cloves, peeled and finely sliced
4 shallots, peeled and cut into wedges
225 g/8 oz mixed wild mushrooms, such as chanterelles, girolles and morels, wiped and sliced in half if large
2 Tbsp rice wine
2 Tbsp light soy sauce
2 Tbsp chopped fresh basil

TO SERVE
Warm crusty bread, tossed green and mixed pepper salad

SQUID WITH ASSORTED PEPPERS

SQUID NEEDS ONLY A MINIMAL AMOUNT OF COOKING, ESPECIALLY IF IT IS SMALL.
IT IS BETTER TO SLIGHTLY UNDERCOOK; IF OVERCOOKED IT BECOMES CHEWY AND TOUGH.

Serves **3 to 4**
Preparation time **5 minutes**
Cooking time **5 minutes**

450 g/1 lb squid, cleaned and cut into
   rings
1 red pepper, seeded
1 yellow pepper, seeded
1 orange pepper, seeded
2 medium courgettes, trimmed
1 Tbsp sunflower or groundnut oil
2 Tbsp oyster sauce
1 Tbsp hot chilli sauce
6 Tbsp fish or vegetable stock
1 tsp cornflour

TO SERVE
Thai fragrant rice

Rinse the squid thoroughly and place in a bowl.
Cover with boiling water, leave for 1 minute,
then drain and set aside.

Slice the peppers thinly into rings. Cut each ring
in half, forming half-moon shapes. Cut the
courgettes into thin strips.

Heat the wok until hot and add the oil. Stir-fry
the peppers and courgettes for 2 minutes. Blend
together the oyster and chilli sauce, stock and
cornflour, then pour into the wok and bring to
the boil. Cook for 1 minute and add the squid.
Stir for 1 minute, or until the squid is hot, and
serve immediately with freshly cooked Thai
fragrant rice.

SQUID AND MONKFISH STIR-FRY

IF YOU ARE LUCKY ENOUGH TO BUY YOUR SQUID STILL WITH
THEIR LITTLE TENTACLES ON, USE THEM AS A GARNISH.

Serves **4**
Preparation time **10 minutes plus
  30 minutes marinating time**
Cooking time **6 to 8 minutes**

225 g/8 oz prepared squid
450 g/1 lb angler fish
2 green serrano chillies,
   seeded and chopped
2 garlic cloves, peeled and crushed
2 Tbsp grated lime zest
4 Tbsp lime juice

1 Tbsp groundnut oil
8 spring onions, trimmed and
   diagonally sliced
175 g/6 oz sugar snap peas or mangetout
100 g/4 oz bean sprouts
1 Tbsp Thai fish sauce (nam pla)
2 Tbsp soy sauce
1 Tbsp chopped fresh coriander
1 Tbsp roasted peanuts, optional

TO SERVE
Freshly cooked rice

Rinse the squid and cut into rings if necessary. Remove the central bone
and any skin from the monkfish, and cut into small dice. Place in a shallow
dish. Blend together the chillies, garlic, 1 tablespoon of the lime zest and
the lime juice. Pour over the squid and fish and allow to marinate for at
least 30 minutes.

Heat the wok, add the oil and stir-fry the squid and monkfish for 3 minutes.
Add the spring onions, sugar snap peas or mangetout, and continue to stir-fry
for 1 minute.

Add the bean sprouts to the wok with the Thai fish and soy sauce. Stir-fry
for 2 to 4 minutes or until the fish is tender, and sprinkle with the coriander,
remaining lime zest and peanuts. Serve with freshly cooked rice.

PRAWN WRAPS

I LOVE FAJITAS AND ENJOY USING DIFFERENT INGREDIENTS TO
CREATE A VARIETY OF FLAVOURS WITHIN THE TORTILLA PANCAKES.
THESE ARE AS DELICIOUS AS THEIR MEXICAN COUSINS.

Serves **4 (makes 8 tortillas)**
Preparation time **15 minutes plus 30**
  minutes marinating time
Cooking time **5 minutes**

FOR THE SALSA

4 ripe tomatoes, seeded and chopped
2 spring onions, trimmed and finely
  chopped
1 jalapeño chilli, seeded and finely
  chopped
2 Tbsp lime juice
1 tsp honey, warmed
2 Tbsp chopped fresh coriander

FOR THE WRAPS

6 spring onions, trimmed and shredded
  into matchsticks
7.5 cm/3 in piece cucumber, peeled if
  preferred and cut into thin strips
150 ml/¼ pt soured cream
1 Tbsp sunflower oil
350 g/12 oz raw king prawns, peeled
4 shallots, peeled and sliced into
  thin wedges
1 jalapeño chilli, seeded and thinly sliced
1 red pepper, seeded and thinly sliced
1 green pepper, seeded and thinly sliced
1 to 2 Tbsp dark soy sauce, or to taste
Hot chilli sauce to taste
8 large wheat tortilla pancakes, warmed

Combine all the ingredients for the salsa and spoon into a small bowl. Cover and
let stand for 30 minutes to allow the flavours to develop.

Place the shredded spring onions, cucumber and soured cream in serving bowls;
cover until required.

Heat the wok and add the oil. When hot, add the king prawns, shallots and chilli
and stir-fry for 2 minutes. Add the sliced peppers and continue to stir-fry for 2 to
3 minutes, or until the prawns have turned pink. Add soy sauce and hot chilli
sauce to taste. Place on a warmed serving dish and serve.

To eat, spread a warmed tortilla pancake with a little soured cream, top with the
prawn and pepper mixture, some spring onions and cucumber, and finally a
spoonful of salsa. Sprinkle with black pepper, and roll up to eat.

Prawn Wraps

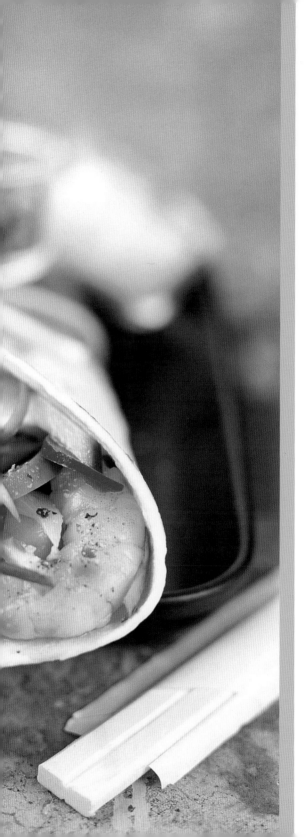

PRAWNS WITH CRISP RICE

MAKE SURE THE RICE IS THOROUGHLY DRY BEFORE FRYING.
EITHER DRY IN AN OVEN ON A BAKING SHEET OR LEAVE ON
PAPER TOWELS OVERNIGHT.

Serves **4**
Preparation time **8 minutes**
Cooking time **8 to 10 minutes**

225 g/8 oz green beans, trimmed and cut
   into small pieces
350 g/12 oz raw prawns, peeled but
   tail shell left on
3 Tbsp cornflour
1 large egg white
300 g/10 oz cold cooked white rice
About 300 ml/½ pt oil for deep-frying

1.25 cm/1 in piece root ginger,
   peeled and shredded
1 yellow pepper, seeded and diced
225 g/8 oz can water chestnuts, sliced
2 Tbsp light soy sauce
2 to 4 tsp hot chilli sauce, or to taste
1 tsp honey
5 Tbsp fish or vegetable stock

TO GARNISH
3 spring onions, trimmed and finely
   chopped

Blanch the beans in boiling water for 3 minutes, drain and set aside. Lightly rinse
the prawns and pat dry with paper towels. Blend the cornflour with the egg white.
Toss the prawns in the egg white mixture and set aside.

Heat the oil in the wok to 190°C/375°F. Pat the rice dry with paper towels and
carefully add it to the oil. (You may find it easier to do this in batches.) The rice will
sizzle and puff up very quickly. Remove, drain on paper towels and set aside.

Drain the wok, wipe clean and reheat. Add 1 tablespoon of the drained oil and stir-fry
the ginger for 30 seconds. Add the prawns and stir-fry for 2 to 3 minutes or until they
change colour. Remove from the wok with a slotted spoon and set aside.

Add another tablespoon of oil and stir-fry the yellow pepper, green beans and
water chestnuts for 2 to 3 minutes.

Return the prawns to the wok with the soy and chilli sauces, the honey and the
stock. Stir-fry for 1 to 2 minutes, or until the beans are tender. Serve with the
crisp rice, sprinkled with the spring onions.

SCALLOP AND ORANGE STIR-FRY

SESAME OIL IS A THICK, RICH GOLDEN-BROWN OIL WITH A DISTINCTIVE NUTTY FLAVOUR. BECAUSE IT HEATS VERY RAPIDLY AND BURNS EASILY, IT IS OFTEN ADDED AT THE END OF COOKING TO ROUND OFF THE FLAVOUR OF A DISH.

Rinse the scallops, discard the black vein if still present and cut in half. Place in a shallow dish and pour the soy sauce, honey and orange juice over it. Stir lightly, cover and allow to marinate in the refrigerator for at least 30 minutes.

Cut the broccoli into small florets and place in a bowl, cover with boiling water, let stand for 5 minutes then drain and set aside.

Cut the celery, carrot and orange pepper into thin strips and set aside.

When ready to cook, drain the scallops, setting aside 2 tablespoons of the marinade. Heat the wok until hot and add the oil. When hot, stir-fry the celery and carrot strips for 2 minutes. Add the scallops and stir-fry for 1 minute before adding the drained broccoli florets and spring onions. Add the marinade and continue to stir-fry for 2 minutes, or until the scallops and vegetables are just tender. Add the sesame oil and stir lightly. Serve sprinkled with the orange zest and with freshly cooked noodles.

Serves **4**
Preparation time **10 minutes**
Cooking time **5 to 7 minutes**

12 large scallops
3 Tbsp light soy sauce
1 tsp honey, warmed
2 Tbsp orange juice
175 g/6 oz broccoli florets
3 celery stalks, trimmed
1 large carrot, peeled
1 orange pepper, seeded
1 Tbsp sunflower or vegetable oil
6 spring onions, trimmed and
   sliced diagonally
1 tsp sesame oil

TO GARNISH
Grated orange zest

TO SERVE
Freshly cooked noodles

SALMON WITH SPRING VEGETABLES

WHEN CUTTING THE SALMON INTO STRIPS, TRY TO REMOVE
AS MANY SMALL BONES AS POSSIBLE.

Serves **4**
Preparation time **10 minutes plus
  30 minutes marinating time**
Cooking time **6 minutes**

450 g/1 lb salmon fillets
1 serrano chilli, seeded and chopped
1 Tbsp grated lime zest
1 Tbsp grated lemon zest
2 Tbsp lemon juice
1 Tbsp lime juice

225 g/8 oz carrots, scrubbed
100 g/4 oz mangetout
175 g/6 oz baby asparagus spears
225g/8 oz stir-fry rice noodles
2 Tbsp groundnut oil
2 Tbsp light soy sauce
2 tsp sesame oil
2 Tbsp pine nuts

TO GARNISH
Lemon and lime zest

Cut the salmon fillets into cubes, place in a shallow dish and scatter the chopped chilli over. Blend the lime and lemon zest and juices together and pour over the salmon. Cover and marinate in the refrigerator for at least 30 minutes, longer if time permits.

Cut the carrots into thin matchsticks, the mangetout and the asparagus spears in half and set aside.

Cover the noodles with boiling water and leave for 4 minutes, or until soft. Drain and set aside.

Heat the wok until hot and add 1 tablespoon groundnut oil. Drain the salmon, setting aside the marinade and stir-fry for 1 minute. Remove from the wok and set aside.

Add the remaining groundnut oil to the wok. When hot, add the prepared vegetables and stir-fry for 2 minutes. Return the salmon to the wok with marinade. Stir-fry for another 1 to 2 minutes, or until the fish is done. Sprinkle with the soy sauce, sesame oil and pine nuts. Stir for 30 seconds and serve immediately with the noodles, garnished with lemon and lime zest.

Salmon with Spring Vegetables

STEAMED TROUT WITH
OYSTER SAUCE

OYSTER SAUCE IS A THICK BROWN SAUCE MADE FROM
A CONCENTRATE OF OYSTERS COOKED IN SOY SAUCE
AND BRINE. IT DOES NOT TASTE FISHY AND IS USED BOTH
IN COOKING AND AS A CONDIMENT. ONCE OPENED,
KEEP IN THE REFRIGERATOR.

Serves **4**
Preparation time **10 minutes**
Cooking time **13 to 15 minutes**

1 Tbsp groundnut oil
1 to 2 tsp dried crushed chillies
2 Tbsp light soy sauce
1 Tbsp rice wine or dry sherry
3 Tbsp oyster sauce
2 Tbsp orange juice
4 small trout, cleaned

2 tsp roasted seasoning,
  (see page 24)
7.5 cm/3 in piece root ginger, peeled
  and thinly sliced
2 spring onions, trimmed and
  finely shredded
Grated zest of 1 orange

TO SERVE
Radish rosettes and shredded
  pak choi

Heat the wok until hot and add the oil; heat until almost smoking. Stir-fry the
chillies for 30 seconds. Add the soy sauce, rice wine or sherry, oyster sauce and
orange juice and stir well until blended. Pour into a small pan and keep warm.
Wipe the wok clean.

Clean the trout and sprinkle the cavity with the roasted seasoning. Place the thinly
sliced ginger inside the cavities and put the trout in a bamboo steaming basket.
Scatter with a few of the shredded spring onions. Cover with the lid.

Fill the wok with boiling water to a depth of 10 cm/4 in. Place the basket into
the wok and steam the trout for 12 to 15 minutes, or until done.

Remove the trout from the bamboo basket and place on a warmed serving platter.
Scatter with the remaining shredded spring onions and orange zest. Gently warm
the sauce and pour over the fish. Garnish and serve.

SEAFOOD STIR-FRY WITH
HABAÑERO SALSA

THIS SALSA WILL WORK WELL WITH MANY OF THE RECIPES IN THIS BOOK. MAKE IT AHEAD OF TIME
TO ALLOW THE FLAVOURS TO DEVELOP. IF DESIRED, THE PAPAYA CAN BE SUBSTITUTED WITH MANGO.

Combine all the ingredients for the salsa and place in a serving bowl. Cover, and let stand for 30 minutes to allow the flavours to develop.

Cut the broccoli into small florets and blanch in boiling water for 5 minutes. Drain and pat dry with paper towels.

Cut the salmon into small pieces, discarding as many of the pin bones as possible. Remove the thin black vein if necessary from the scallops and cut in half if large.

Heat the wok and add the oil. Stir-fry the salmon and scallops for 1 minute. Add the broccoli and continue to stir-fry for 2 minutes, then add the soy sauce and honey. Continue to stir-fry for 1 to 3 minutes, or until the fish is done. Serve immediately with freshly cooked egg noodles.

Serves **4**
Preparation time **20 minutes**
   plus 30 minutes marinating time
Cooking time **4 to 6 minutes**

FOR THE SALSA

**1 ripe papaya, peeled, seeded
   and diced**
**4 spring onions, trimmed and
   finely chopped**
**1 to 2 habañero chillies, seeded
   and finely chopped**
**3 ripe tomatoes, seeded and
   finely chopped**
**1 to 2 tsp dark brown sugar,
   or to taste**
1 Tbsp chopped fresh coriander
2 tsp grated lime zest

FOR THE STIR-FRY

225 g/8 oz broccoli florets
225 g/8 oz salmon fillet
225 g/8 oz scallops, cleaned
1 Tbsp groundnut oil
2 Tbsp light soy sauce
1 tsp honey

TO SERVE

**Freshly cooked medium
   egg noodles**

SWEET-AND-SOUR SEA BASS

IF YOU CANNOT FIND SEA BASS FILLETS, USE OTHER FILLETS SUCH AS TROUT OR MULLET.

Soak the seaweed in lukewarm water, drain, dry thoroughly and set aside.

Rinse the fish and pat dry with paper towels. Sprinkle the fillets with the Chinese five-spice powder and leave for 30 minutes, then coat in the cornflour.

Meanwhile make the sauce. Place all the sauce ingredients, except the cornflour into a small saucepan. Bring to the boil, simmer for 1 minute and blend the cornflour with 1 tablespoon water. Stir into the sauce, and continue to stir until slightly thickened. Set aside.

Heat the oil for deep-frying in the wok to 190°C/350°F. Place the seaweed in a frying basket and deep-fry for 20 to 30 seconds, or until crisp. Drain on paper towels and set aside. Reheat the oil if necessary.

Place the carrots and courgettes in a wire basket and deep-fry for about 30 seconds, or until crisp. Remove and drain on paper towels. Deep-fry the spring onions for 10 to 20 seconds, drain and set aside. Reheat the oil if necessary.

Place 2 to 3 fillets in the hot oil and deep-fry for 3 to 4 minutes, or until crisp and golden. Drain on paper towels and keep warm. Repeat until all the fillets are cooked and reheat the sauce, if necessary. Arrange the fish fillets on a bed of seaweed on the serving plates, pour over a little of the sauce and top with the deep-fried vegetables. Garnish with the radishes and the spring onions.

Serves **4**
Preparation time **10 minutes plus**
30 minutes marinating time
Cooking time **6 to 8 minutes**

25 g/1 oz dried seaweed
4 to 8 sea bass fillets, depending on size
2 tsp Chinese five-spice powder
2 Tbsp cornflour
1 carrot, peeled and shredded
1 large courgette, peeled and shredded
6 spring onions, trimmed and shredded
About 300 ml/¹⁄₂ pt oil for deep-frying

FOR THE SAUCE

1 large shallot, peeled and chopped
1 garlic clove, peeled and chopped
150 ml/¹⁄₄ pt fish or chicken stock
2 Tbsp dark soy sauce
1 Tbsp tomato purée
1 Tbsp rice vinegar or white
   wine vinegar
1 Tbsp honey
1 to 2 tsp cornflour

TO GARNISH

Radish rosettes and shredded
   spring onions

DEEP-FRIED PRAWN PLATTER

SOY SAUCE IS ONE OF THE MOST ESSENTIAL INGREDIENTS OF ASIAN COOKING. IT IS MADE FROM A MIXTURE OF SOYA BEANS, FLOUR AND WATER THAT HAS BEEN FERMENTED AND AGED.

Blend the soy sauce with the honey and ½ tsp of chillies and set aside. Peel the prawns, leaving the tail shell on but removing the heads and the thin black vein that runs down the back of the prawn. Place in a shallow dish.

Blend together the remaining chillies, lemon juice and chopped coriander, and pour over the prawns. Stir lightly, cover and marinate in the refrigerator for 30 minutes, stirring occasionally.

Cover the broccoli florets with boiling water and leave for 10 minutes. Drain and pat dry with paper towels. Set aside. Cut the peppers into 1.25-cm/2-in strips and set aside.

When ready to cook, beat the egg, cornflour and 1 tablespoon water to form a thin batter and stir in the sesame oil. Heat the oil in the wok to 180°C/350°F. Dip the prawns into the batter, allowing any excess to drip back into the bowl. Deep-fry about 4 of the prawns for 2 minutes, or until golden. Drain on paper towels. Repeat until all the prawns have been cooked.

Dip a few broccoli florets and pepper strips into the batter. Deep-fry in the wok for 2 to 3 minutes, or until golden. Drain on paper towels. Repeat until all the vegetables have been cooked.

Arrange the prawns and vegetables on a platter. Serve with rice, a green salad and a small bowl of soy sauce for dipping,

Serves **4**
Preparation time **10 minutes plus 30 minutes marinating time**
Cooking time **15 minutes**

3 Tbsp light soy sauce

1 tsp honey, warmed

1 tsp dried crushed chillies

350 g/12 oz raw king prawns

3 Tbsp lemon juice

2 Tbsp chopped fresh coriander

175 g/6 oz small broccoli florets

1 red pepper, seeded

1 yellow pepper, seeded

1 large egg

2 Tbsp cornflour

2 tsp sesame oil

300 ml/½ pt oil for deep-frying

TO SERVE

Freshly cooked rice, green salad and soy sauce

LOBSTER AND MANGO MEDLEY

IF FRESH COOKED LOBSTER IS UNAVAILABLE, USE RAW PRAWNS ON THEIR OWN OR A COMBINATION OF PRAWNS AND SCALLOPS.

Serves **4**
Preparation time **8 to 10** minutes
Cooking time **6 minutes**

1 Tbsp groundnut oil
½ to 1 habañero chilli, seeded and chopped
1.25 cm/1 in piece root ginger, peeled and grated
450 g/1 lb cooked fresh lobster meat, cubed
300 g/10 oz fresh raw large prawns, peeled

5 spring onions, trimmed and diagonally sliced
1.25 cm/1 in piece cucumber, peeled if preferred and diced
1 large ripe mango, peeled, pitted and diced
2 Tbsp light soy sauce
2 Tbsp lime juice
1 Tbsp grated lime zest
2 Tbsp chopped fresh basil

TO SERVE
Freshly cooked Thai fragrant rice and pak choi salad

Heat the wok, add the oil and stir-fry the chilli and ginger for 1 minute. Add the lobster and/or prawns and stir-fry for 3 minutes. Add the spring onions, cucumber and mango and stir-fry for another 2 minutes.

Add the soy sauce, lime juice and zest stir-fry for 1 minute, or until the prawns are done and the lobster piping hot. Sprinkle with the basil and serve with freshly cooked Thai fragrant rice and a salad of pak choi.

MONKFISH WITH SPINACH AND PEPPERS

YOU CAN USE ANY WHITE FISH FILLETS, SCALLOPS, OR RAW KING PRAWNS FOR THIS DISH. USE THE TOTAL QUANTITY STATED FOR THE MONKFISH.

Serves **4**
Preparation time **10 minutes**
Cooking time **8 to 10 minutes**

675 g/1 lb monkfish
2 Tbsp seasoned flour
2 Tbsp groundnut oil
5 cm/2 in piece root ginger, peeled and shredded into very thin strips
1 to 2 bird's eye chillies, seeded and shredded
2 to 4 garlic cloves, peeled and thinly shredded
1 red pepper, seeded and shredded

1 green pepper, seeded and shredded
225 g/8 oz fresh spinach, shredded
1 Tbsp Thai fish sauce (nam pla)
2 Tbsp oyster sauce
1 Tbsp black bean sauce
225 g/8 oz fresh spinach, shredded
1 tsp sesame oil
4 spring onions, trimmed and diagonally sliced

TO SERVE
Freshly cooked white and wild rice

Cut the fish into cubes and toss them in the seasoned flour. Set aside. Heat the wok, add 1 tablespoon of the groundnut oil, and stir-fry the ginger, chillies and garlic for 1 minute.

Add the remaining oil and stir-fry the fish for 2 to 3 minutes, or until sealed. Add the red and green peppers and continue to stir-fry for 2 minutes.

Blend together the fish, oyster and black bean sauces. Pour into the wok and cook for 2 minutes. Add the spinach and stir-fry for 1 minute, or until the fish is done. Add the sesame oil and stir-fry for 30 seconds. Serve immediately, sprinkled with the spring onions, with freshly cooked white and wild rice.

BEEF, PORK
AND **LAMB**

STEAK STRIPS WITH BEAN PESTO

BECAUSE WOK COOKING IS SO QUICK, IT IS IMPORTANT TO BUY THE BEST-QUALITY BEEF
STEAK YOU CAN – ALTHOUGH MARINATING HELPS TO TENDERIZE THE MEAT, IT CANNOT
TENDERIZE CHEAPER CUTS THAT NEED LONG, SLOW COOKING.

Trim the steak and discard any fat or gristle, then cut into thin strips and place in a shallow dish. Grind some black pepper over the top. Blend 1 tablespoon of the oil with the balsamic vinegar and the red wine. Pour over the steak, cover and marinate in the refrigerator for at least 30 minutes.

Meanwhile, make the pesto. Cook the broad beans in lightly salted boiling water for 5 minutes, or until tender. Drain and let stand until cool enough to handle. Remove the beans from their skins and place in a food processor.

Add the garlic cloves, horseradish, lemon zest and juice and blend in short sharp bursts until a rough purée is formed. With the motor running, slowly pour in the 6 tablespoons of olive oil in a thin steady stream until a sauce consistency is formed.

Scrape into a bowl, stir in the Parmesan cheese, mix lightly, and set aside.

Heat a wok, and when really hot, add the remaining tablespoon of oil. Drain the steak and stir-fry for 2 to 4 minutes, or until done to personal preference. Remove with a slotted spoon and drain briefly on paper towels.

Either toss the cooked steak strips in the broad bean pesto until lightly coated and heat through for 30 seconds, or serve the pesto as a dipping sauce with the steak. Accompany with diced roasted potatoes, onion wedges and garlic; garnish with rosemary sprigs.

Serves **4**
Preparation time **15 minutes plus**
  30 minutes marinating time
Cooking time **10 minutes**

450 g/1 lb sirloin steak
Freshly ground black pepper
2 Tbsp olive oil
1 Tbsp balsamic vinegar
4 Tbsp red wine

FOR THE BEAN PESTO
175 g/6 oz shelled broad beans
2 to 4 garlic cloves, peeled and crushed
1 tsp grated horseradish root or creamed
  hot horseradish sauce
1 Tbsp grated lemon zest
2 Tbsp lemon juice
6 Tbsp extra-virgin olive oil
4 to 6 Tbsp freshly grated Parmesan cheese

TO SERVE
Diced roasted potatoes, onion wedges
  and garlic

TO GARNISH
Rosemary sprigs

SPICED BEEF WITH TOMATOES

RIPE FRESH TOMATOES CAN BE USED INSTEAD OF THE CANNED TOMATOES
IN THIS RECIPE THE FLAVOUR IS SUPERB.

Trim the steak, cut into thin strips and place in a shallow dish. Blend the garlic, chillies, Worcestershire sauce and tomato purée with 2 tablespoons water. Add the sugar and pour over the steak. Cover and let stand in the refrigerator for 30 minutes, stirring occasionally.

Heat the wok and add 1 tablespoon of the oil. When hot, stir-fry the onion for 2 minutes. Remove from the wok with a slotted spoon and set aside.

Add the remaining oil to the wok and stir-fry the beef for 3 minutes. Return the onions to the wok and stir in the contents of the can of tomatoes.

Cook, stirring frequently, for 2 to 4 minutes, or until the beef is tender. Serve immediately, sprinkled with the shredded basil, with a tossed green salad and warm crusty bread.

Serves **4**
Preparation time **5 minutes plus 30 minutes marinating time**
Cooking time **9 minutes**

450 g/1 lb beef fillet or sirloin
3 large garlic cloves, crushed
1 tsp dried crushed chillies
1 Tbsp Worcestershire sauce
1 Tbsp tomato purée
1 tsp sugar
2 Tbsp oil
1 onion, peeled and sliced
400 g/14 oz can chopped tomatoes
2 Tbsp shredded fresh basil

TO SERVE
Tossed green salad and warm
crusty bread

TERIYAKI BEEF STIR-FRY

DARK SOY SAUCE HAS BEEN AGED LONGER THAN LIGHT SOY SAUCE AND IS SLIGHTLY THICKER AND STRONGER – IT IS IDEAL TO USE AS A DIPPING SAUCE.

Serves **4**
Preparation time **10 minutes**
   plus 30 minutes marinating time
Cooking time **5 minutes**

450 g/1 lb sirloin steak
4 Tbsp dark soy sauce
4 Tbsp mirin
2 Tbsp sake or sherry
100 g/4 oz sugar snap peas
1 red pepper, seeded

100 g/4 oz baby asparagus
1 Tbsp sunflower oil

TO GARNISH
1 bird's eye chilli, thinly sliced
   and seeded

TO SERVE
Freshly cooked Thai
   fragrant rice

Trim the steak, discarding any fat. Slice thin into flat slices, rather than strips, and place in a shallow dish. Blend the soy sauce, mirin and sake and pour over the steak. Cover and marinate in the refrigerator for at least 30 minutes. Spoon the marinade over occasionally during this time.

Trim the sugar snap peas, slice the red pepper into thin strips, and trim the bases from the asparagus spears and cut into 5 cm/2 in lengths.

When ready to cook, drain the steak, keeping 2 tablespoons of the marinade to one side. Heat the wok and add the oil. Add the prepared vegetables and stir-fry for 1 minute. Remove from the wok and set aside.

Add the drained beef to the wok and stir-fry for 2 minutes. Return the vegetables to the wok with the reserved marinade. Stir-fry for 1 to 2 minutes, or until the beef is done to personal preference and the vegetables are hot but still crisp.

Serve the beef, sprinkled with the chilli, with the Thai fragrant rice.

BEEF STRIPS WITH AUBERGINE

CUT THE AUBERGINE FOR THIS RECIPE INTO SMALL CUBES TO ENSURE THAT THEY ARE COOKED THOROUGHLY.

Serves **4**
Preparation time **10 minutes**
Cooking time **9 to 11 minutes**

450 g/1 lb beef steak, such as
   sirloin or rump
2 Tbsp groundnut oil
1 aubergine, trimmed and diced
225 g/8 oz green beans,
   trimmed, halved, and blanched

1 red pepper, seeded and cut
   into thin strips
3 tomatoes, seeded and chopped
4 Tbsp hoisin sauce
2 Tbsp light soy sauce
1 tsp sesame oil
1 Tbsp chopped fresh
   flat-leaf parsley

Trim the beef if necessary and cut into thin strips. Heat the wok, add 1 tablespoon of the groundnut oil, and stir-fry the beef strips for 2 minutes or until sealed. Remove from the wok with a slotted spoon and set aside.

Add the remaining oil and stir-fry the aubergine for 3 minutes. Add the beans and red pepper and stir-fry for 2 minutes.

Return the beef to the wok together with the tomatoes, hoisin and soy sauce. Continue to stir-fry for 2 to 4 minutes, or until the beef is tender and the vegetables are done but still crisp.

Add the sesame oil, give a final stir, then sprinkle with the parsley and serve.

THAI BEEF PARCELS

CHILLIES ARE USED EXTENSIVELY IN ASIAN COOKERY – THE BIRD'S EYE CHILLI IS EXTREMELY HOT,
SO REMEMBER TO TAKE CARE WHILE HANDLING AND DO WASH YOUR HANDS THOROUGHLY AFTERWARDS
BEFORE TOUCHING ANY PARTS OF THE BODY.

Trim the beef, cut into thin matchsticks and place in a shallow dish. Scatter the chilli, garlic, lemon grass and galangal or ginger over the top. Blend the lime juice with 1 tablespoon of the oil, pour over the beef and stir until coated. Cover and let stand in the refrigerator for at least 30 minutes.

Meanwhile, make the dipping sauce by combining all the ingredients together. Let stand for about 20 minutes to allow the flavours to develop.

Place the coriander, cucumber, spring onions and peanuts in small serving dishes and the lettuce leaves in a basket.

When ready to serve, drain the beef and heat the wok until hot, then add the remaining oil. When hot, stir-fry the beef for 2 to 3 minutes, or until done to personal preference. Arrange on a warmed serving platter. Serve with the dipping sauce and accompaniments.

To eat, place a lettuce leaf on a plate, fill with a spoonful of beef, add a few of the accompaniments. Sprinkle on a little dipping sauce, fold over and eat.

Makes **8 parcels**
Preparation time **20 minutes**
   plus 30 minutes marinating time
Cooking time **3 minutes**

300 g/10 oz sirloin steak
1 to 2 bird's eye chillies, seeded and chopped
2 to 3 garlic cloves, peeled and crushed
2 lemon grass stalks, chopped, outer leaves discarded
2.5 cm/1 in piece galangal or root ginger, peeled and grated
3 Tbsp lime juice
2 Tbsp sunflower oil

FOR THE DIPPING SAUCE
3 Tbsp light soy sauce
¼ tsp hot pepper sauce, or to taste
2 tsp honey, warmed

TO SERVE
2 Tbsp chopped fresh coriander
10 cm/4 in piece cucumber, peeled if preferred and cut into thin matchsticks
6 to 8 spring onions, trimmed and shredded
50 g/2 oz roasted peanuts, chopped
8 to 10 whole large iceberg lettuce leaves, lightly rinsed

ASIAN BEEF

POUND THE STEAK WITH A MEAT MALLET TO TENDERIZE IT BEFORE CUTTING INTO STRIPS.

Cut the beef steak into thin strips and set aside. Heat the wok and add 1 tablespoon of the oil. When hot, stir-fry the beef for 2 minutes, or until sealed. Remove from the wok with a slotted spoon and set aside.

Add the remaining oil to the wok and stir-fry the garlic, celery and carrot for 2 minutes. Add the asparagus and stir-fry for 1 minute.

Return the beef to the wok with the chilli paste and cook for 2 minutes, stirring throughout. Blend the coconut milk and cornflour together, add to the wok and cook, stirring, until the sauce has thickened and the beef is tender. Sprinkle with the coriander. Serve with the rice, garnished with chilli flowers.

Serves **4**
Preparation time **10 minutes**
Cooking time **9 minutes**

550 g/1¼ lb beef steak, such as
   sirloin or fillet
2 Tbsp groundnut oil
2 to 3 garlic cloves, peeled
   and chopped
4 celery sticks, trimmed and
   cut into sticks
2 carrots, peeled and cut into
   thin sticks
100 g/4 oz baby asparagus, trimmed
   and cut in half
2 Tbsp green chilli paste
   (see page 12)
150 ml/¼ pt coconut milk
1 tsp cornflour
2 Tbsp chopped fresh coriander

TO SERVE
Freshly cooked rice

TO GARNISH
Chilli flowers

FIVE-SPICE LAMB

BUY BEAN SPROUTS THE DAY YOU INTEND TO USE THEM AS THEY DO NOT KEEP VERY WELL.

Serves **4**
Preparation time **10 minutes**
Cooking time **7 to 8 minutes**

175 g/6 oz medium egg noodles
450 g/1 lb lean lamb, such as leg
   steaks
2 Tbsp groundnut oil
4 shallots, peeled and cut
   into wedges
3 garlic cloves, peeled and sliced
1 bird's eye chilli, seeded
   and chopped
1 red pepper, seeded and sliced
   into half-moons
1 large courgette, trimmed and
   cut into thin strips
2 tsp Chinese five-spice powder
1 Tbsp dark soy sauce
1 Tbsp honey
3 Tbsp lamb or chicken stock
1 tsp cornflour
4 oz bean sprouts
6 spring onions, trimmed and
   diagonally sliced

Cook the noodles in boiling water for 4 minutes, or according to the packet instructions. Drain and set aside.

Trim the lamb if necessary and cut into small strips. Heat the wok, add 1 tablespoon of the oil, and stir-fry the lamb for 3 minutes or until sealed. Remove from the wok and set aside.

Add the remaining oil to the wok and stir-fry the shallots, garlic and chilli for 1 minute. Add the red pepper and courgette and continue to stir-fry for 2 minutes. Then return the lamb to the wok.

Blend the Chinese five-spice powder with the soy sauce, honey, stock and cornflour and stir into the wok. Cook, stirring, then stir in the reserved noodles and the bean sprouts. Cook for 1 to 2 minutes or until the lamb is tender, then serve sprinkled with the spring onions.

THAI-STYLE SPICY PORK

WHEN I SERVED THIS TO MY DAUGHTER WHO HAS TRAVELLED EXTENSIVELY IN ASIA, SHE THOUGHT IT TASTED AS AUTHENTIC AS ANY DISH SHE HAD EATEN ON HER TRAVELS.

Serves **4**
Preparation time **8 minutes**
Cooking time **7 to 8 minutes**

1 Tbsp groundnut oil
2 shallots, peeled and chopped
2 garlic cloves, peeled
   and chopped
1 lemon grass stalk, chopped,
   outer leaves discarded
1 to 2 bird's eye chillies, seeded
   and chopped
2 Tbsp grated root ginger
2 kaffir lime leaves
225 g/8 oz fresh pork fillet,
   cut into thin strips
100 g/6 oz baby asparagus
   spears, halved
1 yellow pepper, seeded
   and sliced
1 Tbsp Thai fish sauce (nam pla)
2 Tbsp plum sauce
3 Tbsp coconut milk
8 spring onions, trimmed
   and chopped
2 Tbsp chopped fresh coriander

TO SERVE
Freshly cooked noodles

Heat the wok, add the oil and stir-fry the shallots, garlic, lemon grass, chillies and root ginger for 1 minute. Add the lime leaves and pork and continue to stir-fry for 2 to 3 minutes, or until the pork is sealed.

Add the asparagus and yellow pepper strips and continue to stir-fry for 2 minutes. Stir in the fish and plum sauce with the coconut milk, stir-fry for 2 minutes, then add the spring onions and chopped coriander and serve with the noodles.

LAMB WITH RED PEPPERS AND CHERRY TOMATOES

LAMB FILLET IS IDEAL FOR STIR-FRYING BECAUSE THE FAT IN IT HELPS TO MAKE THE MEAT TENDER, AND ALSO GIVES IT A REALLY GOOD FLAVOUR.

Serves **4**

Preparation time **10 minutes plus 30 minutes marinating time**

Cooking time **8 minutes**

450 g/1 lb lamb fillet

4 garlic cloves, peeled and crushed

2 Tbsp sunflower oil

4 Tbsp chopped fresh flat-leaf parsley

1 Tbsp tomato purée

3 Tbsp orange juice

2 red peppers, seeded and sliced thin

100 g/4 oz cherry tomatoes, halved

50 g/2 oz pitted black olives, halved

Salt and freshly ground black pepper

TO SERVE

Fresh rocket leaves

Trim off any excess fat from the fillet, cut into thin strips and place in a shallow dish. Blend the garlic with 1 tablespoon oil, 2 tablespoons parsley, the tomato purée and the orange juice, then pour over the lamb. Turn the fillet. Cover and marinate in the refrigerator for at least 30 minutes.

Heat the wok until hot, add the remaining 1 tablespoon oil and stir-fry the peppers for 2 minutes. Remove from the wok.

Add the lamb and marinade to the wok and stir-fry for 3 minutes before returning the peppers to the wok. Stir-fry for 60 seconds and add the cherry tomatoes and olives. Stir-fry for 1 to 2 minutes or until the lamb is tender. Add seasoning to taste and serve on a bed of rocket leaves, sprinkled over with the remaining parsley.

THAI BEEF CURRY

LEMON GRASS IS A LONG SLIM BULB WITH A DISTINCTIVE LEMON-CITRUS FLAVOUR. CUT OFF THE ROOT TIP AND PEEL AWAY THE TOUGH OUTER LAYERS OR LEAVES. LEMON GRASS WILL KEEP FOR SEVERAL DAYS IN A COOL PLACE AND CAN BE CHOPPED AND FROZEN.

Serves **4**

Preparation time **5 minutes**

Cooking time **9 minutes**

1 Tbsp oil

3 Tbsp red chilli paste (see page 12)

2 lemon grass stalks, chopped, outer leaves discarded

450 g/1 lb beef fillet or sirloin, trimmed and cubed

1 green pepper, seeded and cut into strips

1 red pepper, seeded and cut into strips

150 ml/¼ pt beef stock

2 Tbsp lime juice

1 to 2 tsp Thai fish sauce (nam pla)

1 to 2 tsp dark brown sugar

TO GARNISH

2 Tbsp roasted peanuts, chopped

1 Tbsp chopped fresh coriander

TO SERVE

Freshly cooked Thai fragrant rice

Heat the wok then add the oil and stir-fry the red chilli paste and lemon grass over a low heat for 2 minutes. Increase the heat slightly then add the beef and stir-fry for 3 minutes.

Add both the peppers and continue to stir-fry for 2 minutes before adding the stock, lime juice, fish sauce and sugar. Continue to stir-fry for 2 minutes or until the beef is tender.

Serve, sprinkled with the chopped peanuts and coriander, with the freshly cooked rice.

CHILLI LAMB

GROUNDNUT OIL IS WIDELY USED IN ORIENTAL COOKING, BECAUSE IT HAS A MILD, PLEASANT TASTE AND CAN BE HEATED TO A HIGHER TEMPERATURE THAN OTHER OILS, WHICH MAKES IT PERFECT FOR DEEP- AND STIR-FRYING. IF YOU CANNOT FIND THIS OIL, USE EITHER CORN OR SUNFLOWER OIL.

Discard any excess fat or gristle from the lamb, cut into thin strips and place in a shallow dish. Blend the garlic, chillies, coriander lime juice, tomato purée and 1 tablespoon of the oil and pour over the lamb. Stir well, cover and marinate in the refrigerator for 30 minutes. Stir occasionally during this time.

Place the green pepper in a small bowl, cover with boiling water and let stand for 5 minutes, then drain and set aside.

When ready to cook, heat the wok and add the remaining oil. Stir-fry the lamb for 3 minutes, then add the drained green pepper and the kidney beans and stir-fry for 2 minutes.

Meanwhile cover the noodles with boiling water, leave for 4 minutes, then drain and keep warm.

Add the cherry tomatoes to the wok and stir-fry for 2 to 3 minutes, or until the tomatoes have began to break up and the lamb is tender. Add seasoning to taste. Serve the lamb with the noodles, the soured cream, salsa and grated cheese. Sprinkle with chopped flat-leaf parsley.

Serves **4**
Preparation time **10 minutes plus 30 minutes marinating time**
Cooking time **8 minutes**

450 g/1 lb lamb fillet
3 garlic cloves, peeled and crushed
1 to 2 red serrano chillies, seeded and chopped
1 tbsp chopped fresh coriander
2 Tbsp lime juice
2 Tbsp tomato purée
2 Tbsp groundnut oil
1 green pepper, seeded and chopped
400-g/14-oz can red kidney beans, drained and rinsed
25 g/8 oz medium egg noodles
175 g/6 oz cherry tomatoes, halved
Salt and freshly ground black pepper

TO SERVE
Soured cream, salsa, grated Cheddar or Monterey Jack cheese and flat-leaf parsley

LAMB LIVER WITH RED PEPPER AND SHERRY

LIVER IS IDEAL COOKING IN A WOK AS IT ONLY NEEDS A MINIMUM OF COOKING, AND WITH A WOK THERE IS LESS DANGER OF THE LIVER BEING OVERCOOKED.

Serves **4**
Preparation time **10 minutes**
Cooking time **8 minutes**

175 g/6 oz broccoli florets

450 g/1 lb lamb liver

2 Tbsp cornflour

2 Tbsp oil

1 red onion, peeled and sliced into rings

1 red pepper, seeded and cut into half-
   moon slices

2 garlic cloves, peeled and sliced

3 Tbsp medium-dry sherry

2 Tbsp light soy sauce

1 tsp honey

Cover the broccoli with boiling water and leave
for 5 minutes, then drain and set aside.

Discard any tubes from the liver and cut into
strips, rinse lightly and pat dry on paper towels.
Coat in the cornflour and set aside.

Heat the wok and add 1 tablespoon of the oil. Then
add all the vegetables, including the garlic, and
stir-fry for 3 minutes. Remove with a slotted
draining spoon and set aside.

Add the remaining oil to the wok and stir-fry the
lamb liver for 2 minutes. Return the vegetables
to the wok and stir-fry for 2 minutes before
adding the sherry, soy sauce and honey; stir-fry for
1 minute. Serve immediately.

LAMB STIR-FRY
WITH OYSTER SAUCE

THIS COLOURFUL DISH WOULD BE PERFECT FOR AN
INFORMAL SUPPER OR LUNCH.

Serves **4**
Preparation time **10 minutes**
Cooking time **10 to 11 minutes**

450 g/1 lb lean lamb

1 Tbsp roasted seasoning
   (see page 24)

1 Tbsp groundnut oil

1 red onion, peeled and cut into wedges

2 to 4 garlic cloves, peeled and
   sliced thin

1 red pepper, seeded and
   thinly sliced

1 orange pepper, seeded
   and thinly sliced

2 Tbsp light soy sauce

4 Tbsp oyster sauce

200 g/7 oz pak choi, shredded

6 spring onions, trimmed and
   diagonally sliced

TO SERVE
Freshly cooked noodles

Trim the lamb of all its fat and cut into thin strips. Place in a plastic bag
with the seasoning and toss until lightly coated.

Heat the wok and add the oil. When hot, stir-fry the lamb for 4 minutes. Add
the onion and garlic and continue to stir-fry for 1 minute.

Add the red and orange peppers and continue to stir-fry for 3 minutes before
adding the soy and oyster sauce. Stir-fry for 1 to 2 minutes, or until the lamb
is tender, then add the shredded pak choi and cook for 1 minute. Sprinkle
with the spring onions and serve with the noodles.

HONEYED PORK

WHEN USING HONEY IN A RECIPE FOR A MARINADE, IT IS ALWAYS A GOOD IDEA TO WARM THE HONEY BRIEFLY BEFORE MEASURING IT OUT. YOU CAN EITHER DO THIS IN A MICROWAVE FOR A FEW SECONDS, OR IF THE OVEN IS ON, PLACE THE JAR ON THE OVEN SHELF. ALTERNATIVELY, PLACE THE JAR IN A BOWL AND POUR SOME BOILING WATER AROUND IT TO COME HALFWAY UP THE SIDES. LET STAND FOR ABOUT 1 MINUTE, THEN USE.

Cut the pork into thin strips and place in a shallow dish. Blend the honey, hoisin sauce, ginger and crushed garlic with 2 tablespoons boiling water and pour over the pork. Cover and marinate for 30 minutes in the refrigerator.

Heat the wok, add the oil and stir-fry the pork for 2 minutes, or until sealed. Add the carrot to the wok and continue to stir-fry for another 2 minutes before adding the mushrooms, soy sauce and rice wine or dry sherry.

Stir-fry for 2 minutes, and then add the shredded pak choi, the water chestnuts and the bamboo shoots. Cook for another 1 to 2 minutes, or until the pork is tender. Add the parsley and serve with freshly cooked noodles.

Serves **4**
Preparation time **8 to 10 minutes plus 30 minutes marinating time**
Cooking time **7 to 8 minutes**

450 g/1 lb pork fillet
2 Tbsp honey
1 Tbsp hoisin sauce
1 Tbsp grated root ginger
1 garlic clove, peeled and crushed
1 Tbsp groundnut oil
2 carrots, peeled and cut into matchsticks
100 g/4 oz shiitake mushrooms, wiped and sliced
2 Tbsp light soy sauce
1 Tbsp rice wine or dry sherry
200 g/7 oz pak choi, shredded
225-g/8-oz can water chestnuts, drained
225-g/8-oz can bamboo shoots, drained
1 Tbsp chopped fresh flat-leaf parsley

TO SERVE
Freshly cooked noodles

STIR-FRIED PORK WITH MANGO

FRESH ROOT GINGER IS A STAPLE INGREDIENT IN ASIAN CUISINE. IT IS ESPECIALLY USEFUL WHEN COOKING SEAFOOD AS IT HELPS TO NEUTRALIZE FISH ODOUR. KEEP IN THE REFRIGERATOR FOR UP TO 2 WEEKS, WRAPPED IN PLASTIC WRAP.

Serves **4**
Preparation time **10 minutes**
  plus 30 minutes marinating time
Cooking time **8 minutes**

450 g/1 lb pork fillet
5 cm/2 in piece root ginger,
  peeled and grated
1 green jalapeño chilli, seeded
  and chopped
2 large garlic cloves, peeled
  and crushed
5 Tbsp mango or orange juice
2 Tbsp dark soy sauce
2 Tbsp oil

6 shallots, peeled and cut
  into fine shreds
2 courgette, trimmed and
  cut into strips
1 red pepper, seeded and cut
  into thin strips
1 ripe but firm mango, peeled,
  pitted, and cut into strips

TO GARNISH
Grated orange zest

TO SERVE
Freshly cooked white rice

Trim the pork, cut into strips, and place in a shallow dish. Scatter the ginger, chilli and garlic over the pork, then pour over the fruit juice, soy sauce and 1 tablespoon of the oil. Cover and leave in the refrigerator for 30 minutes, stirring occasionally. Drain the pork and set aside the marinade.

When ready to serve, heat the wok and add the remaining oil. When heated, stir-fry the pork for 4 minutes. Add the shallots, courgette and red pepper and stir-fry for 2 minutes. Add the mango and stir-fry for 1 minute, or until the pork is tender.

Add the remaining marinade, stir-fry for 1 minute, then sprinkle with the orange zest and serve with the rice.

SWEET-AND-SOUR PORK BITES

USE PORK FILLET FOR THIS DISH AND CUT INTO BITE-SIZE PIECES, TRIMMING OFF ANY EXCESS FAT OR SINEW.

Trim the pork, cut into small cubes, and place in a shallow dish. Blend the soy sauce with the roasted seasoning and the vinegar. Pour over the pork, stir, cover and marinate in the refrigerator for at least 30 minutes. Stir the pork a few times while marinating. Heat the oil in the wok to 190°C/375°F.

Meanwhile, beat the egg, then beat in the cornflour until a thin batter is formed. Remove the pork from the marinade and coat, a few pieces at a time, in the batter. Fry in the hot oil for 3 minutes, or until golden and cooked. Drain on paper towels. Repeat until all the pork has been cooked. Place in a serving dish and keep warm.

Place all the sauce ingredients in a medium-sized pan, stirring well to blend in the cornflour. Place over a moderate heat and cook, stirring until slightly thickened. Serve with the pork, garnishing with the chives.

Serves **4**
Preparation time **10 minutes**
   plus 30 minutes marinating time
Cooking time **12 minutes**

350 g/12 oz lean pork
1 Tbsp light soy sauce
½ to 1 tsp roasted seasoning,
   or to taste (see page 24)
1 Tbsp rice wine or sherry
1 medium egg
2 Tbsp cornflour
Groundnut or sunflower oil for
   deep-frying

FOR THE SAUCE
½ small red pepper, seeded and
   cut into thin strips
1 small carrot, peeled, cut into
   thin ribbons
1 Tbsp sherry vinegar
1 Tbsp tomato paste
1 Tbsp soy sauce
1 tsp light brown sugar
120 ml/4 fl oz chicken stock
1 tsp honey
1 to 2 tsp cornflour

TO SERVE
Freshly cooked rice

TO GARNISH
Chives

PORK WITH GREEN VEGETABLES
AND CRISP NOODLES

IT IS AMAZING TO WATCH THESE NOODLES PUFF UP IN THE HOT OIL. DO TAKE CARE THOUGH:
IF YOU LEAVE THEM IN FOR TOO LONG, THEY QUICKLY GET BURNT.

Blanch the broccoli in boiling water for 5 minutes, then drain
and set aside.

Heat the oil for deep-frying in the wok to 190°C/375°F. Carefully
place a few noodles in the oil for 10 to 20 seconds or until puffed up
and golden, then remove and drain. Repeat until all the noodles
are cooked.

Trim the pork, cut into thin strips and set aside. Heat the wok, then
add 1 tablespoon of the groundnut oil and stir-fry the garlic, ginger
and lemon grass for 1 minute. Add the remaining groundnut oil and
stir-fry the pork until sealed. Add the broccoli and continue to
stir-fry for 2 minutes.

Add the remaining vegetables and stir-fry for 2 to 3 minutes,
then add the soy sauce, fish sauce and honey. Stir-fry for
2 minutes, or until the pork is tender and the vegetables are done
but still crisp. Serve with the crisp noodles.

Serves **4**
Preparation time **15 minutes**
Cooking time **8 to 9 minutes**

175 g/6 oz broccoli florets

450 ml/¾ pt oil for deep-frying

2 to 3 oz cellophane (transparent
   stir-fry) noodles

450 g/1 lb pork fillet

2 Tbsp groundnut oil

2 garlic cloves, peeled and chopped

5 cm/2 in piece root ginger, peeled
   and shredded

1 lemon grass stalk, chopped, outer
   leaves discarded

1 small courgette, trimmed and
   cut into strips

100 g/4 oz sugar snap peas or
   mangetout

8 spring onions, trimmed and
   diagonally sliced

2 Tbsp light soy sauce

1 Tbsp Thai fish sauce (nam pla)

1 tsp honey

PORK WITH BLACK BEAN SAUCE

ASIAN COOKERY INVOLVES A NUMBER OF THICK, FLAVOURFUL SAUCES SUCH AS BLACK BEAN SAUCE. IT IS MADE FROM SALTED BLACK BEANS OR BLACK SOYA BEANS WHICH HAVE BEEN FERMENTED WITH SALT AND SPICES. THE SAUCE HAS A DISTINCTIVE, SLIGHTLY SALTY TASTE WITH A HINT OF GARLIC AND FRESH GINGER.

Trim the pork and cut into very thin strips. Blend the soy sauce with the orange juice and cornflour in a large bowl. Add the pork and toss until coated. Cover lightly and let stand in the refrigerator for at least 30 minutes to marinate.

Heat the wok until hot and add 1 tablespoon of the oil. When hot stir-fry the garlic for 30 seconds. Add the pork and stir-fry for 2 minutes. Remove from the wok and set aside.

Wipe the wok clean if necessary and heat the remaining oil, then add the carrot, 2 spring onions, green beans and cucumber and stir-fry for 2 minutes. Return the pork to the wok, add the black bean sauce, and stir-fry for 1 to 2 minutes, or until the pork is tender.

Serve with the freshly cooked noodles, sprinkled with the remaining spring onions.

Serves **4**
Preparation time **10 minutes plus 30 minutes marinating time**
Cooking time **5 to 6 minutes**

450 g/1 lb pork fillet
1 Tbsp light soy sauce
1 Tbsp orange juice
1 tsp cornflour
2 Tbsp groundnut or sunflower oil
3 garlic cloves, peeled and sliced thin
1 large carrot, peeled and cut into very thin strips
3 spring onions, trimmed and sliced
100 g/4 oz green beans, trimmed and halved
5 cm/2 in piece cucumber, peeled if preferred and cut into strips
3 to 4 Tbsp black bean sauce

TO SERVE
Freshly cooked medium egg noodles

PORK SPRING ROLLS

IF PREFERRED YOU CAN REPLACE THE BEAN SPROUTS WITH THE SAME AMOUNT OF FINELY
SHREDDED PAK CHOI.

Cut the pork into very fine strips and place in a shallow dish.
Blend together the soy sauce, rice wine or sherry and cornflour.
Pour over the pork and let stand for 30 minutes.

Heat the wok, add the groundnut oil and stir-fry the pork for
1 minute. Add the sesame oil, chilli and vegetables and stir-fry for
another 2 to 3 minutes. Remove and cool.

Blend the flour with 2 to 3 tablespoons water to form a paste
then place a spring roll wrapper on the work counter and place
2 to 3 tablespoons of the filling on the wrapper. Brush the edges
with a little of the flour paste and turn the edges into the centre.
Roll up to encase the filling and seal the edge with the flour paste.
Press the edges firmly. Repeat until all the wrappers and filling
have been used. (If using phyllo pastry, fold a sheet of pastry in half
and then in half again, brushing the pastry with a little water before
folding. Proceed as for spring roll wrappers.)

Heat the wok, add the oil for deep-frying, and heat to 190°C/375°F.
Deep-fry 3 to 4 rolls at a time for 3 minutes or until crisp. Turn the
rolls over during cooking. Drain well on paper towels. Repeat until
all the rolls are cooked and serve warm.

Serves **4 to 6**
Preparation time **20 minutes plus**
  30 minutes marinating time
Cooking time **12 to 16 minutes**

225 g/8 oz lean pork fillet
2 Tbsp soy sauce
1 Tbsp rice wine or dry sherry
1 tsp cornflour
1 Tbsp groundnut oil
1 Tbsp sesame oil
1 bird's eye chilli, seeded and
  finely chopped
1 orange pepper, seeded
  and cut into thin shreds
100 g/4 oz carrot, peeled and grated
75 g/3 oz bean sprouts
100 g/4 oz water chestnuts,
  shredded
4 Tbsp plain flour
1 packet spring roll wrappers
  or about 12 sheets phyllo pastry
Groundnut oil for deep-frying

POULTRY
AND **GAME**

FRAGRANT CHICKEN

KAFFIR LIME LEAVES ARE SMOOTH, DARK GREEN LEAVES WITH AN INTENSELY AROMATIC CITRUS-PINE FLAVOUR. THEY CAN BE FROZEN AND CAN BE BOUGHT DRIED AS WELL. IF UNAVAILABLE, USE GRATED LIME ZEST.

Make 3 diagonal slashes across each chicken breast and place in a shallow dish.

Place the lemon grass, cardamom pods, dried crushed chillies, lime leaves, spring onions, star anise and coriander in a food processor and blend to a chunky purée or pound to a purée in a pestle and mortar. Stir in the lime zest and juice and spread over the chicken breast. Cover and let stand in the refrigerator for 30 minutes.

Heat the wok and add the oil. When hot, cook the chicken for 5 minutes, turning frequently, until browned. Add the stock, reduce the heat and cover with either a lid or large piece of foil.

Cook for 15 minutes, or until the chicken is thoroughly cooked. Serve with the cooking juices spooned over and garnished with the chilli and spring onions.

Serves **4**
Preparation time **5 minutes plus
   30 minutes marinating time**
Cooking time **20 minutes**

**4 boneless, skinless chicken
   breast fillets**
**3 lemon grass stalks, chopped, outer
   leaves discarded**
6 cardamom pods, lightly crushed
½ to 1 tsp dried crushed chillies
**3 kaffir lime leaves, crushed if
   using dried leaves**
6 spring onions, trimmed and chopped
3 star anise
1 Tbsp chopped fresh coriander
1 Tbsp grated lime zest
2 Tbsp lime juice
1 Tbsp oil
250 ml/8 fl oz chicken stock

TO GARNISH
**Shredded chilli and chopped
   spring onions**

CHICKEN WITH PEANUT SAUCE

PALM SUGAR IS A BROWN SUGAR WITH A CARAMEL FLAVOUR. IT IS SOLD IN BLOCKS – A GOOD
SUBSTITUTE IS DARK BROWN SUGAR.

Heat the wok, add 2 tablespoons of the oil and gently stir-fry
the garlic, ginger and chillies for 1 minute. Add the peanuts
and stir-fry for 4 to 5 minutes or until the peanuts are golden.
Add the sugar and the stock, bring to the boil and simmer
for 5 minutes.

Remove from the heat, cool slightly, then transfer to a food
processor and blend to form a purée. Set aside. Wipe the
wok clean.

Heat the wok again, add the remaining oil and stir-fry the
chicken for 3 minutes or until sealed. Add the peanut sauce
and the lime juice and cook for 4 to 6 minutes, stirring until
the chicken is thoroughly cooked. Sprinkle with the chilli and
serve with the lime wedges.

Serves **4**
Preparation time **10 minutes**
Cooking time **20 minutes**

3 Tbsp oil
1 garlic clove, peeled and crushed
2.5 cm/1 in piece root ginger,
  peeled and grated
1 to 2 bird's eye chillies, seeded
  and chopped
100 g/4 oz raw shelled peanuts

2 tsp palm sugar or
  dark brown sugar
300 ml/$^1\!/_2$ pt chicken or
  vegetable stock
450 g/1 lb boneless, skinless
  chicken breast fillets, cut into
  small cubes
2 Tbsp lime juice

TO SERVE
Sliced red chilli and lime wedges

SWEET-AND-SOUR CHICKEN
WITH FRIED RICE

THIS IS QUITE A SUBSTANTIAL DISH AND UNLIKE SOME OF THE OTHER RECIPES, IT DOES NOT NEED MANY ACCOMPANYING DISHES. ONE THAT IS GOOD WITH THIS WOULD BE STIR-FRIED CUCUMBER (SEE PAGE 91).

Cook the rice in lightly salted water for 12 minutes, or until the rice is tender. Drain and set aside.

Heat the wok and add 1 tablespoon of the oil. When hot, stir-fry the chicken for 2 to 3 minutes or until sealed.

Add the carrot and green pepper and continue to stir-fry for 2 minutes. Stir in the pineapple, honey, sweet chilli sauce, vinegar and soy sauce. Continue to stir-fry for another 2 minutes or until the chicken is done. Remove from the wok and set aside.

Wipe the wok clean if necessary. Add the remaining oil to the wok, and add the cooked rice with the peas and red pepper. Cook for 3 to 4 minutes or until hot. Return the chicken to the wok with the spring onions. Heat through, stirring, for 2 minutes or until piping hot, and serve immediately.

Serves **4**
Preparation time **10 minutes**
Cooking time **23 to 25 minutes**

175 g/6 oz long-grain rice

Salt to taste

2 Tbsp groundnut oil

350 g/12 oz fresh chicken stir-fry strips

1 large carrot, peeled and diced

1 green pepper, seeded and chopped

4 slices fresh or canned pineapple, chopped

2 Tbsp honey, warmed

1 to 2 Tbsp sweet chilli sauce, or to taste

3 Tbsp rice wine vinegar or white wine vinegar

2 Tbsp dark soy sauce

100 g/4 oz frozen peas

1 small red pepper, seeded and finely chopped

6 spring onions, trimmed and chopped

CHICKEN WITH SPICED YOGHURT SAUCE

ADDING THE GROUND ALMONDS AT THE END OF THE COOKING TIME
HELPS TO THICKEN THE SAUCE AS WELL AS GIVING A SLIGHT NUTTY FLAVOUR.

Heat the wok, add 1 tablespoon of the oil and stir-fry the chicken for 3 to 4 minutes or until sealed. Remove from the wok and set aside.

Reheat the wok. Add the remaining oil and stir-fry the onion, garlic and chillies for 1 minute. Return the chicken to the wok, add the spices and continue to stir-fry for 1 minute.

Add the stock and cook for 5 minutes before adding the yoghurt and ground almonds. Heat gently for 2 to 3 minutes, stirring frequently, then sprinkle with the chopped coriander and almonds. Garnish with lemon wedges and serve with rice.

Serves **4**
Preparation time **5 minutes**
Cooking time **14 minutes**

2 Tbsp oil
450 g/1 lb boneless, skinless chicken breasts, cut into strips
1 onion, peeled and cut into wedges
3 to 4 garlic cloves, peeled and thinly sliced
2 green jalapeño chillies, seeded and chopped
1 tsp ground cumin
1 tsp ground coriander
6 green cardamom pods, bruised
150 ml/¼ pt chicken stock
150 ml/¼ pt low-fat, plain yoghurt
2 Tbsp ground almonds
2 Tbsp chopped fresh coriander
1 Tbsp toasted flaked almonds

TO GARNISH
Lemon wedges

TO SERVE
Freshly cooked rice

ASIAN-STYLE CHICKEN

MIRIN IS A RICE WINE USED FOR COOKING, NOT DRINKING.
IT ADDS A SWEET FLAVOUR. IF UNAVAILABLE, USE SHERRY.

Serves **4**
Preparation time **10 minutes plus 30**
minutes marinating time
Cooking time **40 minutes**

One 1.5 kg/3 lb chicken, jointed into
8 portions
1 Tbsp mirin or dry sherry
2 Tbsp dark soy sauce
1 tsp dried crushed chillies
2.5 cm/1 in piece root ginger,
peeled and chopped
2 tsp roasted seasoning
(see page 24)
2 tsp palm or dark brown sugar

FOR THE SAUCE
2 Tbsp Chinese chilli sauce
3 Tbsp light soy sauce
1 Tbsp sesame oil
1 tsp honey, warmed
2 Tbsp mirin or dry sherry

TO GARNISH
Chopped chives

TO SERVE
Stir-fried red and green pepper strips
and shredded spring onions

Remove and discard the chicken skin, score the flesh and set aside. Blend
the mirin or sherry, soy sauce, dried crushed chillies, ginger, seasoning and
sugar, and rub over the chicken portions. Leave in the refrigerator for at least
30 minutes, longer if time permits.

Place either a steamer or a rack in the wok and add 5 centimetres/2 inches of
water. Arrange the chicken on an ovenproof plate and bring the water to the boil.
Cover the wok tightly with either a lid or foil and gently steam the chicken for
about 30 minutes, or until it is tender. Add more water to the wok if required.

Just before cooking, combine all the ingredients for the sauce and set aside.

Serve with the sauce, garnished with chives and stir-fried vegetables.

Asian-style Chicken

MARINATED STIR-FRY CHICKEN

THAI BASIL IS DARKER THAN ITS EUROPEAN COUNTERPART AND THE FLAVOUR IS MORE EARTHY. IF UNAVAILABLE, USE ORDINARY (SWEET) BASIL.

Serves **4**
Preparation time **10 minutes plus 30 minutes marinating time**
Cooking time **9 minutes**

350 g/12 oz boneless, skinless chicken breasts
½ to 1 tsp dried crushed chillies
2 Tbsp olive oil
3 Tbsp orange juice
A few sprigs of fresh basil

1 Tbsp groundnut oil
1 red onion, peeled and cut into wedges
1 red pepper, seeded and cut into small chunks
400-g/14-oz can artichoke hearts, drained and cut in half
Assorted bitter salad leaves, such as watercress, rocket and mustard greens

Trim the chicken and cut into cubes. Place in a shallow dish and sprinkle with the dried crushed chillies. Blend the olive oil with the orange juice and pour over the chicken. Chop a few sprigs of basil and scatter them over the chicken. Stir, then cover and marinate in the refrigerator for 30 minutes.

Heat the wok and add the groundnut oil. Stir-fry the onion and pepper for 2 minutes. Remove from the wok with a slotted spoon.

Drain the chicken, reserving the marinade, and stir-fry for 3 minutes. Return the red onion and pepper to the wok with the marinade and artichoke hearts. Stir-fry for 2 to 3 minutes, or until the chicken is done. Arrange on the salad leaves and serve.

SIZZLING CHICKEN WITH CASHEWS

MARINATING CHICKEN OR ANY POULTRY IN BEATEN EGG WHITE AND CORNFLOUR TENDERIZES THE MEAT REALLY QUICKLY, AND TRANSFORMS THE TASTE AND ENJOYMENT OF THE DISH.

Serves **4**

Preparation time

 5 minutes plus 30 minutes marinating time

Cooking time **8 minutes**

1 large egg white

1 Tbsp cornflour

450 g/1 lb chicken stir-fry strips

2 Tbsp groundnut oil

1 green serrano chilli, seeded and chopped

3 garlic cloves, peeled and thinly sliced

75 g/3 oz cashews

2 Tbsp light soy sauce

2 Tbsp chopped fresh chilli

TO SERVE

Freshly cooked Thai fragrant rice

Beat the egg white and cornflour together in a medium sized bowl. Add the chicken strips and stir until coated. Cover and leave in the refrigerator for 30 minutes.

When ready to cook, heat the wok until hot and add 1 tablespoon of the oil. Heat for 30 seconds, then stir-fry the chilli and garlic for 1 minute.

Heat the remaining oil, add the chicken strips to the wok and stir-fry for 3 minutes. Add the cashews and continue to stir-fry for 2 to 3 minutes, or until the chicken is done.

Add the soy sauce and stir lightly. Sprinkle with the chopped chilli and serve immediately with rice.

DEEP-FRIED SHREDDED DUCK

THIS DISH IS ABSOLUTELY DELICIOUS AND EXTREMELY QUICK TO PREPARE.

Serves **4**

Preparation time **8 to 10 minutes**

Cooking time **3 to 6 minutes**

350 g/12 oz boneless, skinless duck
  breasts

1 Tbsp hot chilli sauce

1 Tbsp hoisin sauce

4 Tbsp plum sauce

1 Tbsp sesame oil

1 medium egg

1 large carrot, peeled and
  cut into thin matchsticks

1 green pepper, seeded
  and cut into thin strips

3 Tbsp cornflour

300 ml/$\frac{1}{2}$ pt oil for deep-frying

FOR THE DIPPING SAUCE

3 Tbsp plum sauce

1 Tbsp light soy sauce

1 tsp hot chilli sauce or to taste

1 bird's eye chilli, seeded
  and finely chopped

TO GARNISH

Diagonally sliced spring onions

TO SERVE

**Freshly cooked stir-fried
  vegetables and noodles**

Cut the duck into fine shreds and set aside. Place all the other ingredients, except the oil for deep-frying, in a large bowl and stir until blended. Stir in the shredded duck.

Heat the oil in the wok to 190°C/375°F and deep-fry spoonfuls of the mixture in the hot oil for 1 to 2 minutes, breaking up with a spoon to keep the shreds separate. Drain thoroughly. (Do this in 2 to 3 batches.)

Blend the dipping sauce ingredients together. Garnish the duck with spring onions and serve with stir-fried vegetables, noodles and dipping sauce.

STIR-FRIED DUCK WITH PLUM SAUCE

CHINESE FIVE-SPICE POWDER IS A BLEND OF STAR ANISE, SZECHUAN PEPPERCORNS, FENNEL, CLOVES AND CINNAMON. IT WILL KEEP INDEFINITELY IN A SEALED JAR IN A COOL DARK PLACE.

Serves **4**
Preparation time **10 minutes plus 30 minutes marinating time**
Cooking time **25 minutes**

4 duck breasts
2 Tbsp soy sauce
1 tsp Chinese five-spice powder
4 Tbsp orange juice

450 g/1 lb fresh plums, pitted and quartered
1 cinnamon stick, bruised
3 Tbsp light brown sugar
2 Tbsp white wine vinegar
1 Tbsp oil

TO SERVE
Warmed Chinese pancakes, shredded spring onions and cucumber

Discard the skin from the duck breasts. Cut into very thin strips and place in a shallow dish. Blend the soy sauce, Chinese five-spice powder and orange juice, then pour over the duck. Cover and let stand in the refrigerator for 30 minutes.

Rinse the plums and place in the wok with the cinnamon stick, sugar, vinegar and water. Bring to the boil and then simmer for 20 minutes, or until done. Cool and blend to a smooth purée in a food processor. If necessary, pass through a fine sieve to remove any lumps. Set aside.

Wipe the wok clean, then heat. When hot, add the oil. Drain the duck and stir-fry for 3 to 5 minutes, or until done to personal preference. Serve with the warmed pancakes, the shredded spring onions and cucumber and the plum dipping sauce.

Stir-fried Duck with Plum Sauce

TOM YUM SUPPER

THIS SOUP-LIKE DISH IS SO FILLING THAT IT MAKES AN IDEAL
LUNCH OR SUPPER. SERVE WITH SOME WARM STRIPS
OF PITTA OR CRUSTY BREAD.

Serves **4**
Preparation time
  8 to 10 minutes
Cooking time **22 to 23 minutes**

225 g/8 oz boneless, skinless chicken
  breasts
1 l/³⁄₄ pt chicken stock
75 g/3 oz long-grain rice
1 bird's eye chilli, seeded and chopped
2 lemon grass stalks, chopped, outer
  leaves discarded

2 to 3 Tbsp red chilli paste (see page 12)
1 red pepper, seeded and finely
  shredded
1 large carrot, peeled and cut into
  julienne strips
2 Tbsp lime juice
1 to 2 tsp palm or dark brown sugar
100 g/4 oz bean sprouts
1 Tbsp shredded fresh basil leaves

Cut the chicken into thin shreds and set aside. Place the stock in a wok with the
rice, chilli and lemon grass and simmer for 15 minutes. Blend the chilli paste with
a little of the hot stock and stir into the wok together with the chicken, red
pepper, carrot and lime juice.

Simmer the chicken for 5 minutes, then stir in the remaining ingredients (except
the basil) and simmer for 2 to 3 minutes, or until piping hot. Serve in large bowls,
sprinkled with the shredded basil.

TURKEY WITH CRANBERRIES AND SHIITAKE MUSHROOMS

IF FRESH OR FROZEN CRANBERRIES ARE UNAVAILABLE, USE 3 TO 4 TABLESPOONS OF STORE-BOUGHT CRANBERRY SAUCE, PREFERABLY ONE THAT INCLUDES WHOLE CRANBERRIES.

Serves **4**

Preparation time **5 minutes plus 30 minutes**
  marinating time

Cooking time **16 minutes**

75 g/3 oz fresh or defrosted frozen cranberries

1 to 2 Tbsp dark brown sugar, or to taste

450 g/1 lb turkey stir-fry strips

150 ml/¼ pt cranberry juice

2 Tbsp dark soy sauce

1 Tbsp grated orange zest

1 Tbsp groundnut oil

2 garlic cloves, peeled and crushed

100 g/4 oz shiitake mushrooms, wiped and halved

100 g/4 oz sugar snap peas

Place the cranberries and sugar in the wok with 3 to 4 tablespoons water and cook gently for 10 minutes or until the cranberries 'pop'. Remove from the wok and set aside. (Add sufficient sugar to sweeten slightly while still leaving a slight tartness.) Wipe the wok clean.

Place the turkey stir-fry strips in a shallow dish. Blend the cranberry juice with the soy sauce and orange zest and pour over the turkey. Cover and marinate in the refrigerator for at least 30 minutes.

When ready to cook, heat the wok and add the oil. Stir-fry the garlic for 1 minute. Drain the turkey, reserving 2 tablespoons of the marinade. Add the turkey to the wok and stir-fry for 2 minutes.

Add the mushrooms and sugar snap peas to the wok with the reserved marinade and stir-fry for 2 minutes. Add the cooked cranberries and stir-fry for 1 minute, or until the turkey is done and the cranberries are hot. Serve immediately.

TWICE-COOKED TURKEY WITH
ASPARAGUS AND MUSHROOMS

THERE ARE MANY VARIETIES OF NOODLES FROM WHICH TO CHOOSE. I WOULD THOROUGHLY RECOMMEND THAT YOU BUY A SELECTION TO TRY. FOR THIS DISH, A BROAD RIBBON EGG NOODLE IS IDEAL.

Serves **4**

Preparation time **8 to 10 minutes**

Cooking time **8 to 10 minutes**

450 g/1 lb turkey breast steaks

150 ml/¼ pt turkey or chicken stock

2 Tbsp groundnut oil

1 red pepper, seeded and sliced

175 g/6 oz asparagus spears,
  cut into 8 cm/3 in lengths

100 g/4 oz shiitake mushrooms,
  wiped and halved

100 g/4 oz oyster mushrooms, wiped
  and halved

5 Tbsp yellow bean sauce

2 Tbsp light soy sauce

1 Tbsp hot chilli sauce, or to taste

1 Tbsp chopped fresh coriander

TO SERVE

Freshly cooked noodles

Cut the turkey into thin strips. Place the stock in the wok and bring to the boil. Add the turkey and cook gently for 3 minutes. Remove from the heat, drain and set aside.

Wipe the wok clean and reheat, then add the oil. When hot, add the drained turkey and stir-fry for 2 to 3 minutes before adding the pepper, asparagus and mushrooms. Stir-fry for 2 minutes. Add the yellow bean, soy and hot chilli sauces.

Stir-fry for 1 to 2 minutes, or until the turkey is done. Sprinkle with the coriander and serve with noodles.

CHICKEN WITH SESAME SEEDS

THERE ARE MANY VARIETIES OF RICE WINE VINEGAR USED IN ASIAN COOKING.
THEY RANGE IN FLAVOUR FROM SPICY AND TART TO SWEET AND PUNGENT.

Cut the chicken into fine shreds, then beat together the egg white and cornflour. Pour the mixture over the chicken and stir lightly until coated. Cover and leave in the refrigerator for at least 30 minutes.

Cut the peppers into fine strips and set aside.

When ready to cook, heat the wok and add 2 tablespoons of the groundnut oil. Add the chicken and stir-fry for 2 to 3 minutes, or until the chicken becomes white. Remove from the wok and set aside. Wipe the wok clean if necessary. Add the remaining oil and the peppers and stir-fry for 1 minute.

Remove with a slotted spoon and set aside.

Reheat the wok and add the sesame oil. Stir-fry the sesame seeds for 1 minute, or until golden. Add all the sauce ingredients and cook for 1 to 2 minutes, stirring frequently.

Return the chicken and peppers to the wok. Stir-fry for 2 minutes, or until the chicken is done.

Serve the chicken with the sauce.

Serves **4**
Preparation time **10 minutes**
  plus 30 minutes marinating time
Cooking time **10 minutes**

450 g/1 lb chicken stir-fry strips
1 large egg white, beaten
1 Tbsp cornflour
1 red pepper, seeded
1 orange pepper, seeded

3 Tbsp groundnut oil
1 tsp sesame oil
1 Tbsp sesame seeds

FOR THE SAUCE

1 Tbsp light soy sauce
1 to 2 tsp hot chilli sauce
2 tsp honey, warmed
1 tsp rice wine vinegar
  or sherry vinegar

LEMON CHICKEN

TO BRUISE LEMON GRASS, ROLL ALONG ITS LENGTH WITH A ROLLING PIN UNTIL THE STALKS
ARE SLIGHTLY CRUSHED. THIS RELEASES ITS WONDERFUL CITRUS AROMA.

Place the broccoli florets in a small bowl. Cover with boiling water, let stand for 5 minutes, then drain and set aside.

Cut the chicken into bite-size cubes and place in a shallow dish. Blend 2 tablespoons of the lemon juice with the cornflour and pour over the chicken. Stir lightly until the chicken is coated. Cover and let stand for 30 minutes in the refrigerator.

When ready to cook, heat the wok and add 2 tablespoons of the oil. Add the chicken and stir-fry for 2 minutes, or until the chicken is white. Remove from the wok and wipe the wok clean.

Return the wok to the heat. When hot add the remaining oil and stir-fry the chilli and lemon grass for 1 minute. Return the chicken to the wok with the broccoli and continue to stir-fry for 2 minutes. Add the remaining lemon juice, soy sauce, rice wine or sherry, the spring onions and the pine nuts and stir-fry for 2 minutes, or until the chicken is thoroughly cooked. Discard the lemon grass stalks and serve immediately, garnished with the lemon zest.

Serves **4**
Preparation time **10 minutes**
  plus 30 minutes marinating time
Cooking time **7 minutes**

225 g/8 oz broccoli florets
450 g/1 lb boneless, skinless
  chicken pieces
4 Tbsp lemon juice
1 Tbsp cornflour
3 Tbsp groundnut oil
1 bird's eye chilli, seeded and
  sliced

2 lemon grass stalks, bruised
2 Tbsp light soy sauce
2 Tbsp rice wine or
  medium-dry sherry
6 spring onions, trimmed and
  diagonally sliced
2 Tbsp toasted pine nuts

TO GARNISH
Grated lemon zest

SZECHUAN TURKEY STIR-FRY

ROOT GINGER CAN BE PREPARED IN SEVERAL DIFFERENT WAYS. YOU CAN GRATE THE GINGER ON THE COARSE SIDE OF A GRATER WITHOUT PEELING IT FIRST, OR YOU CAN PEEL IT AND PASS IT THROUGH A GARLIC PRESS, OR SIMPLY SHRED IT VERY FINELY. WHATEVER YOUR PREFERENCE, THERE'S NO SURPASSING THE FRESH, TANGY FLAVOUR IT IMPARTS TO ANY DISH IN WHICH IT IS USED.

Cut the turkey into thin strips and place in a shallow dish. Scatter with ginger, garlic and chilli over it. Pour in the vinegar, stir well, cover and marinate in the refrigerator for 30 minutes. Stir occasionally during this time.

Heat the wok and add the oil. When hot, stir-fry the turkey for 2 to 3 minutes or until sealed. Add the carrot and sugar snap peas and continue to stir-fry for another 2 minutes.

Blend the black bean sauce with the sweet chilli sauce and honey, and stir the mixture into the wok. Continue to cook, stirring, for 2 to 3 minutes, or until the turkey is done. Sprinkle with the shredded spring onions and serve with fried rice.

Serves **4**
Preparation time **8 minutes plus 30 minutes marinating time**
Cooking time **6 to 8 minutes**

450 g/1 lb turkey breast
2.5 cm/1 in piece root ginger, peeled and grated
3 garlic cloves, peeled and sliced
1 red serrano chilli, seeded and chopped
1 Tbsp rice vinegar
1 Tbsp groundnut oil

1 large carrot, peeled and cut into ribbons
175 g/6 oz sugar snap peas
4 Tbsp black bean sauce
1 to 2 Tbsp sweet chilli sauce to taste
1 tsp honey

TO GARNISH
Shredded spring onions

TO SERVE
Freshly cooked fried rice

VEGETABLES

MUSHROOM AND SUGAR
SNAP PEA STIR-FRY

THIS MAKES AN IDEAL SIDE VEGETABLE DISH. FOR A MORE SUBSTANTIAL MEAL, STIR-FRY SOME DRAINED, CUBED TOFU (BEAN CURD) WITH THE GARLIC AND CHILLI, THEN PROCEED AS BELOW.

Cover the dried mushrooms with almost-boiling water and let stand for 20 minutes before draining. Cut the wild and closed-cup mushrooms in half or quarters, depending on their size, then rinse very lightly and pat dry on paper towels.

Heat the wok and add the oil. When hot, stir-fry the garlic and chilli for 1 minute. Add the orange pepper and stir-fry for 1 minute before adding the mushrooms, including the soaked and drained mushrooms. Continue to stir-fry for 3 minutes. Add the sugar snap peas and stir-fry for 1 minute.

Add the soy and black bean sauces, stir-fry for 2 minutes, and add the spring onions and sesame oil. Stir-fry for 1 minute, or until the vegetables are tender and serve with the rice.

Serves **4**
Preparation time **10 minutes plus 20 minutes soaking time**
Cooking time **9 minutes**

15 g/½ oz dried cep mushrooms
225 g/8 oz assorted wild mushrooms
100 g/4 oz closed cup mushrooms
1 Tbsp oil
4 garlic cloves, peeled and sliced
1 red serrano chilli, seeded and chopped
1 orange pepper, seeded and sliced into half-moon shapes
225 g/8 oz sugar snap peas
2 Tbsp dark soy sauce
4 Tbsp black bean sauce
8 baby spring onions, trimmed
1 tsp sesame oil

TO SERVE
Freshly cooked Thai fragrant rice

STIR-FRIED BROCCOLI
WITH HOISIN SAUCE

WHEN STIR-FRYING BROCCOLI, IT IS A GOOD IDEA TO BLANCH THE BROCCOLI FIRST IN BOILING WATER
SO THAT IT IS COOKED AND TENDER AT THE END OF THE STIR-FRYING TIME.

Cover the broccoli with boiling water and let stand for 5 minutes, then drain and pat dry with paper towels. Cut the orange flesh into segments and set aside.

Heat the wok and add the oil. When hot, add the onion and garlic and stir-fry for 2 minutes.

Add the red pepper and broccoli and continue to stir-fry for 4 minutes. Blend the hoisin sauce with 2 tablespoons water. Stir into the wok and continue to stir-fry for 1 to 2 minutes, or until the broccoli is tender.

Sprinkle in the pine nuts and add the orange segments, give a final stir and serve.

Serves **4 as an accompaniment**
Preparation time **5 minutes plus**
 5 minutes resting time
Cooking time **8 minutes**

350 g/12 oz broccoli florets
1 large orange
1 Tbsp oil
1 red onion, peeled and cut into wedges
2 garlic cloves, peeled and sliced
1 red pepper, seeded and thinly sliced
2 Tbsp hoisin sauce
2 Tbsp roasted pine nuts

STIR-FRIED CABBAGE
WITH SESAME AND GARLIC

COOKING CABBAGE IN THIS WAY KEEPS IT CRISP. COMBINED WITH THE SHALLOTS, GARLIC AND CHILLI, IT MAKES A FLAVOURFUL ACCOMPANIMENT TO GRILLED, PAN-FRIED OR OVEN-BAKED FOODS.

Heat the wok and add 2 teaspoons of the sesame oil. Stir-fry the sesame seeds for 1 to 2 minutes, or until golden. Remove from the wok and set aside.

Cut the bread into small cubes. Reheat the wok and add 2 tablespoons of the oil. Stir-fry the bread cubes for 2 to 3 minutes or until golden; remove from the wok and drain on paper towels.

Wipe the wok clean, reheat and add a further tablespoon of the oil. Stir-fry the garlic, chilli and shallots for 2 minutes. Add the shredded cabbage and stir-fry for 4 minutes, or until almost tender.

Add the remaining sesame oil to the wok, continue to stir-fry for 1 minute, and sprinkle in the reserved sesame seeds and bread croutons. Heat for 30 seconds and serve.

Serves **4**
Preparation time **8 minutes**
Cooking time **10 to 12 minutes**

4 Tbsp sesame oil

2 Tbsp sesame seeds

2 slices white bread

3 to 4 garlic cloves, peeled and sliced

1 red jalapeño chilli, seeded and
  chopped

3 shallots, peeled and cut into
  thin wedges

1 small green cabbage such as Savoy,
  finely shredded

AUBERGINE WITH SHIITAKE MUSHROOMS

SHIITAKE MUSHROOMS ARE AROMATIC BLACK MUSHROOMS THAT ADD A UNIQUE FLAVOUR TO MEAT
AND FISH DISHES. THEY CAN BE BOUGHT DRIED AS WELL AS FRESH, IF DRIED, THEY NEED TO BE
SOAKED FOR AT LEAST 15 MINUTES BEFORE USING.

Serves **4**
Preparation time **10 minutes**
Cooking time **15 minutes**

3 Tbsp oil
1 large onion, peeled and cut into wedges
3 garlic cloves, peeled and sliced
1 red serrano chilli, seeded and chopped
450 g/1 lb aubergine, trimmed and diced
1 red pepper, seeded and sliced
  into half-moon shapes
100 g/4 oz shiitake mushrooms,
  wiped and sliced if large
1 courgette, trimmed and sliced
2 Tbsp dark soy sauce
2 Tbsp mirin or dry sherry

Heat the wok and add 2 tablespoons of the
oil. Stir-fry the onion, garlic and chilli for
2 minutes.

Add the aubergine and stir-fry for 5 minutes over
a moderate heat. Add the remaining oil, the red
pepper, mushrooms, courgette and soy sauce
mirin or dry sherry and continue to stir-fry for
8 minutes, or until the aubergine is tender.
Serve hot.

STIR-FRIED CUCUMBER

COOKED CUCUMBER IS AS DELICIOUS AS RAW.

Serves **4**
Preparation time **10 minutes plus**
  30 minutes marinating time
Cooking time **5 to 6 minutes**

2 large cucumbers
2 tsp salt
1 Tbsp groundnut oil
1 bird's eye chilli, seeded
  and chopped

1 to 2 garlic cloves,
  peeled and chopped
200 g/7 oz pak choi, shredded
4 to 5 Tbsp black bean sauce
8 spring onions, trimmed and
  diagonally sliced
1 tsp sesame seeds

Peel the cucumbers, cut in half lengthways, and scoop out and discard
the seeds. Slice into 1 cm/½ in slices. Place in a colander, and sprinkle
with the salt. Let stand for 30 minutes then rinse in cold water and pat
dry on paper towels.

Heat the wok and add the oil. Stir-fry the chilli and garlic for 2 minutes.
Add the cucumber, stir-fry for 1 minute, then stir in the pak choi and stir-
fry for another 1 minute.

Blend the black bean sauce with 2 tablespoons water and stir into the
wok. Stir-fry for 1 to 2 minutes, or until the pak choi has wilted.

Sprinkle with the spring onions and sesame seeds and serve.

DEEP-FRIED BEANS AND ASPARAGUS

THE BEANS AND ASPARAGUS HAVE A CHEWY TEXTURE AND
WHEN SERVED IN THIS THICK, AROMATIC SAUCE THEY MAKE
A REALLY DIFFERENT BUT DELICIOUS DISH.

Serves **4 as an accompaniment**
Preparation time **5 minutes plus**
 5 minutes soaking time
Cooking time **10 minutes**

225 g/8 oz green beans, trimmed and cut
 in half
225 g/8 oz baby asparagus spears,
 trimmed and cut in half

About 800 ml/½ pt oil for deep-frying
2 garlic cloves, peeled and chopped
1 to 2 green jalapeño chillies,
 seeded and chopped
5 cm/2 in piece root ginger,
 peeled and grated
4 Tbsp yellow bean sauce
1 Tbsp dry sherry

Cover the beans and asparagus with boiling water, let stand for 5 minutes then
drain and pat dry.

Heat the oil in the wok to 180°C/350°F. Deep-fry the beans and asparagus in
small batches for 2 minutes. Remove from the wok with a slotted draining spoon
and drain thoroughly on paper towels.

Drain the oil from the wok, reserving 1 tablespoon, then wipe the wok clean. Add
the oil and stir-fry the garlic, chillies and ginger for 1 minute. Add the fried beans
and asparagus to the wok.

Blend the yellow bean sauce with 2 tablespoons water and pour it into the wok with
the sherry. Cook for 1 to 2 minutes, or until the vegetables are hot. Serve immediately.

Deep-fried Beans and Asparagus

THAI VEGETABLE CURRY

VARY THE TYPE OF SQUASH USED IN THIS CURRY DISH
DEPENDING ON WHICH SQUASHES ARE AVAILABLE.

Serves **4**
Preparation time **10 minutes**
Cooking time **19 to 20 minutes**

1 Tbsp groundnut oil
1 onion, peeled and cut into wedges
450 g/1 lb sweet potatoes, peeled and
   cubed
300 g/10 oz pumpkin, peeled and cubed
1 red pepper, seeded and chopped
1 large courgette, trimmed and
   cut into thick chunks

2 Tbsp red chilli paste (see page 12)
450 ml/³/₄ pt coconut milk
1 Tbsp dark brown sugar
2 Tbsp dark soy sauce
2 Tbsp lime juice

TO GARNISH
Shredded fresh basil leaves

TO SERVE
Freshly cooked Thai rice

Heat the wok and add the oil. When hot, stir-fry the onion, sweet potato and
pumpkin for 4 minutes, until the onion has begun to soften. Add the red pepper
and courgette and continue to cook for 2 minutes.

Blend the chilli paste with the coconut milk and add to the wok with the sugar
and soy sauce. Bring to the boil and simmer for 10 minutes, or until the vegetables
are almost tender.

Add the lime juice and continue to simmer for 3 to 4 minutes, or until the
vegetables are tender. Sprinkle with the shredded basil leaves and serve with
the rice.

WILTED SPINACH WITH GARLIC

FISH SAUCE, AN ESSENTIAL THAI SEASONING, IS A CLEAR BROWN LIQUID, RICH IN
PROTEIN AND B VITAMINS. IT IS SALTY WITH A MILD FLAVOUR.

Discard any tough stems from the spinach, wash thoroughly,
shred then set aside.

Heat the wok, add the oil then stir-fry the garlic and chilli for
1 minute. Add the spinach and stir-fry for 2 to 3 minutes before
adding the tomatoes, spring onions, the soy and fish sauces and
sugar. (You may need to add the spinach in two batches; allow
the first batch to wilt a little before adding the remainder.)

Continue to stir-fry for 1 to 2 minutes, or until the spinach has
wilted, then serve, sprinkled with lemon zest and sliced
almonds, if you like.

Serves **4 as an accompaniment**
Preparation time **5 minutes**
Cooking time **6 minutes**

450 g/1 lb spinach or red chard

1 Tbsp oil

3 garlic cloves, peeled and sliced thin

1 bird's eye chilli, seeded and chopped

3 ripe tomatoes, seeded and chopped

8 spring onions, trimmed and sliced

1 Tbsp dark soy sauce

1 Tbsp Thai fish sauce (nam pla)

1 tsp light brown sugar

1 Tbsp zested lemon rind (optional)

2 Tbsp roasted flaked almonds (optional)

NUTTY SPICY GREENS

USE UNSALTED CASHEWS RATHER THAN THE ROASTED SALTED ONES WHICH
WILL ALTER THE TASTE OF THE DISH.

Heat the wok and add 2 tablespoons of the oil. Stir-fry the cashews for 3 to 4 minutes, or until golden. Remove from the wok with a slotted spoon and reserve.

Add 1 tablespoon of the remaining oil to the wok, heat, and add the onion, garlic, ginger and dried crushed chillies. Stir-fry for 2 minutes.

Add the broccoli, green beans, pepper and mushrooms and stir-fry for 3 minutes. Add the contents of the can of tomatoes, the soy sauce, 2 tablespoons of water and the roasted seasoning.

Continue to cook for 3 to 4 minutes, or until the vegetables are tender. Sprinkle with the cashews and serve with spoonfuls of soured cream or half-fat crème fraîche.

Serves **4**
Preparation time **10 minutes**
Cooking time **11 to 13 minutes**

3 to 4 Tbsp groundnut oil
100 g/4 oz unsalted cashews
1 red onion, peeled and sliced
2 to 3 garlic cloves, peeled
   and chopped
2.5 cm/1 in piece root ginger,
   peeled and finely shredded
½ to 1 tsp dried crushed chillies
225 g/8 oz broccoli florets,
   blanched
175 g/6 oz green beans, trimmed
   and cut into short lengths,
   blanched

1 orange pepper, seeded
   and chopped
100 g/4 oz closed cup mushrooms,
   wiped and halved if large
400 g/14 oz can chopped tomatoes
1 Tbsp dark soy sauce
1 tsp roasted seasoning
   (see page 24), or to taste

TO SERVE
Soured cream or half-fat
   crème fraîche

LENTIL AND RED PEPPER
STIR-FRY

RICE NOODLES ARE TRADITIONALLY EATEN AS AN ALTERNATIVE TO RICE THROUGHOUT
ASIA AND ARE IDEAL TO USE IN BOTH STIR-FRIES AND SOUPS.

Place the broccoli florets in a bowl and cover with boiling water.
Let stand for 5 minutes, then drain and set aside. Cover the
noodles with boiling water, let stand for 4 minutes then drain
and set aside.

Heat the wok and add the oil. Stir-fry the ginger, onion and
garlic for 2 minutes. Add the peppers and drained broccoli and
stir-fry for 3 minutes.

Stir in the drained lentils, cashews, soy sauce, hot chilli sauce
and lime zest and juice. Stir-fry for 1 to 2 minutes, or until the
vegetables are tender. Add the noodles, stir for 1 minute then
sprinkle with sesame seeds and serve.

Serves **4**
Preparation time **15 minutes plus
9 minutes standing time**
Cooking time **8 to 9 minutes**

300 g/10 oz broccoli florets

225 g/8 oz stir-fry rice noodles

1 Tbsp oil

**One small piece root ginger,
peeled and grated**

1 onion, peeled and cut into wedges

3 to 4 garlic cloves, peeled and sliced

2 red peppers, seeded and sliced

300 g/10 oz can green lentils, drained

50 g/2 oz cashews

2 Tbsp dark soy sauce

Few drops hot chilli sauce, or to taste

Grated zest and juice of 1 lime

2 Tbsp sesame seeds

RICE AND NOODLES

PORK WITH CRISPY NOODLES

AFTER USING OIL FOR DEEP FRYING, ALLOW TO COOL, STRAIN IT THROUGH A FINE SIEVE TO REMOVE ANY BITS OF FOOD AND USING A FUNNEL POUR INTO AN EMPTY OIL BOTTLE. SECURE AND LABEL. THIS WAY THE OIL CAN BE USED A FEW TIMES. DO TAKE CARE, HOWEVER, THAT THE OIL IS COOL BEFORE HANDLING.

Soak the noodles in boiling water for 10 minutes, or until soft. Drain and let stand for 10 minutes. (Do this while preparing the meat and vegetables.)

Heat the oil in the wok to 190°C/375°F and deep-fry the noodles in small batches, draining on paper towels. Set aside. Strain off the oil and clean the wok.

Heat the wok again and add 1 tablespoon of the strained oil, then stir-fry the garlic, shallots, chilli and ginger for 1 minute. Add a further tablespoon of oil, then add the pork and stir-fry for 3 minutes.

Add the carrots and peppers and continue to stir-fry for 2 minutes. Add the yellow bean and soy sauces to the wok and continue to stir-fry for 2 minutes, or until the pork is tender. Serve with the crisp noodles.

Serves **4**
Preparation time **10 minutes**
Cooking time **13 minutes**

175 g/6 oz fine egg noodles
450 ml/³⁄₄ pt oil for deep-frying
2 garlic cloves, peeled and crushed
4 shallots, peeled and finely sliced
1 serrano chilli, seeded and chopped
2.5 cm/1 in piece root ginger, peeled and grated
225 g/8 oz pork fillet, trimmed and cut into fine shreds
2 carrots, peeled and cut into julienne strips
1 red pepper, seeded and cut into thin strips
1 green pepper, seeded and cut into thin strips
3 Tbsp yellow bean or black bean sauce
2 Tbsp light soy sauce

EGG-FRIED RICE WITH
CHORIZO SAUSAGE AND PRAWNS

WHEN USING PEELED PRAWNS THAT HAVE ALREADY BEEN COOKED, REHEAT BRIEFLY
AS QUICKLY AS POSSIBLE TO ENSURE THAT THE PRAWNS DO NOT BECOME TOUGH
AND TASTELESS.

Cook the rice in unsalted water for 12 to 15 minutes, or until tender. Drain thoroughly and let stand until cold.

Heat wok and add the oil. When hot, stir-fry the chorizo sausage, Parma ham and peas for 3 minutes.

Add the cold rice, bean sprouts and prawns and stir-fry for 2 minutes, then push to one side of the wok.

Pour the eggs into the base of the wok and stir-fry for 2 minutes over a high heat, or until the eggs have begun to set. Stir in the rice mixture, and continue to cook until the egg has set. Serve immediately, garnished with spring onions and pepper.

Serves **4**
Preparation time **8 minutes**
Cooking time **19 to 22 minutes**

100 g/4 oz long-grain rice
2 Tbsp oil
175 g/6 oz chorizo sausage, diced
50 g/2 oz Parma ham, chopped
100 g/4 oz frozen peas
100 g/4 oz bean sprouts
100 g/4 oz peeled prawns, defrosted if frozen
2 medium eggs, beaten
Salt to taste

TO GARNISH
4 spring onions, trimmed and chopped
Freshly ground black pepper

SPICY BEAN THREAD NOODLES

DRIED PRAWNS GIVE TEXTURE AND AN INTENSE FLAVOUR TO DISHES. THEY CAN BE FOUND
IN ASIAN SPECIALITY FOOD STORES.

Soak the noodles in boiling water for 4 minutes. Drain, and plunge into cold water, then drain again and set aside.

Heat the wok, add 1 tablespoon of the oil, and stir-fry the lemon grass, chillies and ginger for 1 minute. Add the remaining oil then the pork and chicken. Stir-fry for 3 minutes or until sealed.

Add the drained noodles, the fish sauce, sugar, bean sprouts and lime juice and stir-fry for 4 to 5 minutes, or until the noodles are piping hot.

Add the spring onions, coriander and ground prawns if using, and stir-fry for another minute. Serve sprinkled with the peanuts and garnished with the lime wedges.

Serves **4**
Preparation time **10 minutes**
   plus 4 minutes soaking time
Cooking time **9 minutes**

100 g/4 oz cellophane
   (transparent stir-fry) noodles
2 Tbsp oil
3 lemon grass stalks, chopped,
   outer leaves discarded
1 to 2 bird's eye chillies,
   seeded and chopped
2.5 cm/1 in piece root ginger,
   peeled and grated
100 g/4 oz lean pork, cut into thin
   shreds

100 g/4 oz chicken breasts,
   cut into thin shreds
1 Tbsp Thai fish sauce (nam pla)
1 tsp light brown sugar
100 g/4 oz bean sprouts
3 Tbsp lime juice
4 spring onions, trimmed and
   chopped
2 Tbsp chopped fresh coriander
1 Tbsp dried ground prawns,
   optional
1 Tbsp roasted peanuts, chopped

TO GARNISH

Lime wedges

CHICKEN AND PRAWN
CHOW MEIN

LIGHT SOY SAUCE IS SALTIER THAN DARK SOY SAUCE AND IS THE BEST ONE TO USE FOR COOKING.

Cook the noodles in plenty of lightly salted boiling water for 4 minutes, or until tender. Drain, plunge into cold water to cool quickly and set aside.

Shred the chicken into fine strips, place in a shallow dish and pour over the light soy sauce and rice wine or sherry. Let stand for 10 minutes, drain and set aside the marinade.

Heat the wok and add the 2 teaspoons of the oil and heat. Stir-fry the chicken for 2 minutes then remove. Add the remaining oil to the wok; when hot add the garlic and stir for 10 seconds. Add the peas and stir until coated with a little oil. Add the drained noodles, prawns, chicken, reserved marinade and the dark soy sauce.

Stir-fry for 2 minutes. Add the sesame oil, give a final stir and serve immediately, sprinkled with chopped chives.

Serves **4**
Preparation time **5 minutes plus 10 minutes marinating time**
Cooking time **10 minutes**

225 g/8 oz medium egg noodles

100 g/4 oz boneless, skinless chicken breasts

2 Tbsp light soy sauce

1 Tbsp rice wine or dry sherry

1½ Tbsp oil

1 garlic clove, peeled and crushed

75 g/3 oz peas

75 g/3 oz peeled prawns, defrosted if frozen

1 Tbsp dark soy sauce

1 tsp sesame oil

TO GARNISH
Chopped chives

TOFU WITH
PEPPER TRIO AND RICE

TOFU, OR BEAN CURD IS USED EXTENSIVELY IN ASIAN COOKING.
IT IS HIGHLY NUTRITIOUS AND RICH IN PROTEIN. IT HAS A BLAND
TASTE BUT EASILY TAKES ON FLAVOUR WHEN MARINATED.

Serves **4**
Preparation time **10 minutes**
Cooking time **21 minutes**

175 g/6 oz long-grain rice
225 g/8 oz tofu (bean curd)
2 Tbsp oil
3 to 4 garlic cloves, peeled
   and crushed
1 red onion, peeled and cut
   into wedges

1 red pepper, seeded
   and coarsely chopped
1 green pepper, seeded
   and coarsely chopped
1 yellow pepper, seeded
   and coarsely chopped
100 g/4 oz oyster mushrooms,
   wiped and coarsely chopped
4 Tbsp hoisin sauce

Cook the rice in lightly salted boiling water for 12 minutes or until tender, drain
and set aside. Drain the tofu, cut into cubes and set aside.

Heat the wok and add 1 tablespoon of the oil. Fry the tofu with the garlic for
2 minutes, then remove the tofu from the wok with a slotted spoon and set aside.

Add the remaining oil to the wok and stir-fry the onion for 1 minute. Add the
peppers with the mushrooms and stir-fry for 2 minutes, before adding the
hoisin sauce.

Stir-fry for 1 minute, then return the tofu to the wok with the cooked rice and stir-fry
for 3 minutes, or until the vegetables are tender. Serve immediately.

Tofu with Pepper Trio and Rice

PEPPER, CASHEW
AND SUGAR SNAP CHOW MEIN

THIS MAKES A PERFECT ACCOMPANIMENT TO ANY OF THE DISHES
IN THE BOOK OR IS IDEAL AS A MAIN MEAL FOR TWO PEOPLE.

Serves **2 to 4**
Preparation time **8 to 10 minutes**
Cooking time **7 to 9 minutes**

175 g/6 oz medium egg noodles
2 Tbsp groundnut oil
100 g/4 oz unsalted cashews
1 red pepper, seeded and chopped
1 yellow pepper, seeded and chopped

1 orange pepper, seeded and chopped
175 g/6 oz sugar snap peas, trimmed and
  halved
3 Tbsp light soy sauce
1 Tbsp rice wine or dry sherry
1 tsp dark brown sugar
6 spring onions, trimmed and chopped
1 tsp sesame oil

Cook the noodles in plenty of boiling water for 4 minutes, or until cooked tender.
Drain and plunge into cold water to stop them cooking further. Drain and set aside.

Heat the wok and add 1 tablespoon of the groundnut oil. Stir-fry the cashews
for 2 to 3 minutes, or until golden. Remove from the wok and set aside.

Add the remaining oil to the wok, stir-fry the peppers and sugar snap peas for 4
minutes, and then stir in the noodles.

Blend the soy sauce, rice wine or sherry and sugar and pour into the wok.
Stir-fry for 1 to 2 minutes, or until the noodles are hot. Sprinkle with the spring
onions, and cashews, add the sesame oil, give a final stir and serve.

SPECIAL FRIED RICE

THIS IS A USEFUL ACCOMPANIMENT FOR MEAT, FISH OR VEGETABLE DISHES. THERE IS NO HARD AND FAST RULE TO ITS INGREDIENTS – YOU CAN ADD OR SUBTRACT ACCORDING TO PERSONAL PREFERENCE OR WHAT YOU HAVE AVAILABLE.

Serves **4**
Preparation time **5 minutes**
Cooking time **21 to 22 minutes**

225 g/8 oz long-grain rice
2 Tbsp groundnut oil
2 medium eggs, beaten
1 Tbsp.light soy sauce
1 bird's eye chilli, seeded and finely
  chopped
2 Tbsp bacon, chopped
75 g/3 oz peas
175 g/6 oz peeled prawns, defrosted
  if frozen
50 g/2 oz sweetcorn kernels, canned
  or frozen
4 spring onions, trimmed and chopped
Freshly ground black pepper

Cook the rice in lightly salted boiling water for 12 minutes, or until tender. Drain and arrange on a baking sheet to dry.

Heat the wok and add 1 tablespoon of the oil. Beat the eggs with the soy sauce and chilli, pour into the wok and cook until set. Remove the set egg, cool, cut into shreds and set aside.

Wipe the wok clean if necessary, then add the remaining oil to the wok and stir-fry the bacon for 2 minutes.

Add the cooled rice with the peas, prawns and sweetcorn and stir-fry for 3 minutes. Stir in the spring onions and the shredded omelette. Heat for 1 to 2 minutes, or until hot, and serve, sprinkled with black pepper.

FRIED RICE WITH SPICY BEANS

ONCE YOU HAVE ADDED THE EGG, YOU NEED TO STIR THE WOK THOROUGHLY TO ENSURE THAT THE EGG IS COOKED AND DOES NOT MAKE THE RICE SOGGY.

Serves **4 to 6**
Preparation time **5 minutes**
Cooking time **20 minutes**

175 g/3 oz long-grain rice
Salt
2 Tbsp groundnut oil
1 onion, peeled and chopped
2 garlic cloves, peeled
  and chopped
1 red serrano chilli,
  seeded and chopped

1 yellow pepper, seeded and
  chopped
300 g/10 oz canned red kidney
  beans
175 g/6 oz shelled broad beans,
  defrosted if frozen
1 medium egg, beaten
1 Tbsp light soy sauce
2 Tbsp chopped fresh coriander

TO GARNISH
1 tsp paprika

Cook the rice in plenty of lightly salted boiling water for 12 minutes or until tender. Drain and arrange on a baking sheet. Allow to dry.

Heat the wok then add the oil. When hot, stir-fry the onion, garlic and chilli for 2 minutes. Add the yellow pepper and stir-fry for 1 minute, then stir in the cold rice, the red kidney beans and the broad beans. Continue to stir-fry for 3 minutes.

Beat the egg with the soy sauce and pour into the wok. Cook, stirring, for 2 minutes, or until the egg has set. Stir in the coriander and serve sprinkled with the paprika.

KOREAN CELLOPHANE NOODLES WITH MIXED VEGETABLES

IF FRESH KAFFIR LIME LEAVES ARE UNAVAILABLE, LOOK FOR DRIED ONES, THEN SIMPLY CRUMBLE THEM IN WHEN STIR-FRYING THE GARLIC AND CHILLI.

Serves **4**
Preparation time **10 minutes**
Cooking time **8 minutes**

225 g/8 oz cellophane
   (transparent stir-fry) noodles
2 Tbsp groundnut oil
1 to 2 bird's eye chillies, seeded
   and chopped
2 to 4 garlic cloves, peeled
   and chopped
2 lemon grass stalks, chopped,
   outer leaves discarded
2 kaffir lime leaves, crushed

2.5 cm/1 in piece root ginger,
   peeled and finely shredded
2 carrots, peeled and diced
100 g/4 oz broccoli florets
100 g/4 oz cauliflower florets
75 g/3 oz peas
100 g/4 oz baby corn
2 Tbsp dark soy sauce
3 Tbsp oyster sauce
1 Tbsp Thai fish sauce (nam pla)
1 tsp dark brown sugar
1 Tbsp chopped fresh
   basil leaves

Soak the noodles in boiling water for 4 minutes, then drain and set aside.

Heat the wok, add the oil and stir-fry the chillies, garlic, lemon grass, kaffir lime leaves and root ginger for 2 minutes. Add all the vegetables and continue to stir-fry for 3 minutes.

Blend the soy sauce with the oyster and fish sauces, stir in the sugar and add to the wok. Stir, then add the drained noodles.

Continue to cook, stirring, until the vegetables are done but still crisp and the noodles are hot. Sprinkle with the basil leaves and serve.

ORIENTAL NOODLES

ALTHOUGH I HAVE SUGGESTED USING TRANSPARENT NOODLES FOR THIS DISH, OTHER NOODLES WILL WORK AS WELL. JUST FOLLOW THE PACKET INSTRUCTIONS FOR THE LENGTH OF TIME REQUIRED TO SOAK THEM.

Serves **4**
Preparation time **8 minutes**
Cooking time **9 to 11 minutes**

100 g/4 oz cellophane
   (transparent stir-fry) noodles
2 Tbsp groundnut oil
1 medium egg, beaten
2 garlic cloves, peeled
   and chopped
1 bird's eye chilli, seeded
   and chopped

250 g/9 oz tofu (bean curd),
   drained and cubed
2 Tbsp green chilli paste
   (see page 12)
100 g/4 oz bean sprouts
1 Tbsp Thai fish sauce
1 Tbsp sweet chilli sauce
2 Tbsp dark soy sauce
1 Tbsp chopped fresh coriander

Cover the noodles with boiling water, let stand for 4 minutes then drain and set aside.

Heat the wok and add 1 tablespoon of the oil. When hot, pour in the beaten egg and cook until set. Remove the set egg from the wok and cut into strips.

Wipe the wok clean if necessary, reheat then add the remaining oil. Add the garlic and chilli and stir-fry for 1 minute. Add the bean curd and continue to stir-fry for 2 to 3 minutes, or until golden. Add the green chilli paste and stir-fry for another minute. Add the remaining ingredients, except the coriander and the drained noodles. Stir-fry for 3 to 4 minutes or until piping hot. Sprinkle with the coriander, add the noodles and serve.

SALADS

DUCK STRIPS
ON WILTED ROCKET

THIS RECIPE WILL WORK EQUALLY WELL WITH EITHER CHICKEN OR TURKEY BREAST AND MAKES AN INTERESTING MAIN-COURSE SALAD.

Remove 1 tablespoon of the zest from one of the oranges and set aside. Peel the oranges and divide into segments. Remove the skin (over a bowl in order to catch the juice), and set aside the segments.

Trim the duck, cut into thin strips and place in a shallow dish. Blend the orange juice, vinegar and honey together and pour over the duck. Let stand, lightly covered, in the refrigerator for 30 minutes. Stir occasionally during this time.

Heat the wok and add 1 tablespoon of the oil. Drain the duck, reserving the marinade, then stir-fry for 2 minutes or until sealed. Remove from the wok and set aside. If necessary, clean the wok before adding the remaining oil.

Stir-fry the fennel for 2 minutes. Return the duck to the wok with the reserved marinade and stir-fry for 2 minutes. Add the sugar snap peas, cherry tomatoes and rocket or spinach. Stir-fry for 1 to 2 minutes, until the leaves have begun to wilt.

Add the orange segments and give a final stir. Serve immediately with crusty bread or new potatoes.

Serves **4**
Preparation time **10 minutes plus 30 minutes marinating time**
Cooking time **8 to 10 minutes**

2 large oranges
2 duck breasts (about 225 g/8 oz in total)
2 Tbsp orange juice
2 Tbsp balsamic vinegar
1 tsp honey, warmed
2 Tbsp oil
1 fennel head, trimmed and finely sliced
175 g/6 oz sugar snap peas or mangetout, halved
100 g/4 oz cherry tomatoes, halved
225 g/8 oz rocket or baby spinach leaves

TO SERVE
Warm crusty bread or freshly cooked new potatoes

WARM TURKEY SALAD WITH JULIENNED VEGETABLES

THE CRISPY LEEKS FOR THE GARNISH ARE EASY TO MAKE. FINELY SHRED THE LEEKS AFTER CLEANING, AND PLUNGE INTO HOT OIL FOR A FEW SECONDS. DRAIN WELL ON PAPER TOWELS.

Serves **4**
Preparation time
   10 minutes plus 30 minutes
   marinating time
Cooking time **9 to 10 minutes**

300 g/10 oz fresh turkey breast fillet
1 large egg white
1 Tbsp cornflour
3 Tbsp oil
1 small red onion, peeled and thinly sliced

1 red pepper, seeded
   and cut into thin strips
3 Tbsp lemon juice
2 Tbsp dark soy sauce
1 tsp honey

TO SERVE
Frisée salad leaves
Freshly ground black pepper

Trim the turkey, cut into thin strips and place in a shallow dish. Beat the egg white with the cornflour and pour over the turkey. Cover and marinate in the refrigerator for 30 minutes, stirring occasionally.

Heat the wok and add 2 tablespoons of the oil. Stir-fry the turkey for 3 minutes or until sealed. Remove from the wok and set aside. Clean the wok if necessary.

Add the remaining oil to the wok and stir-fry the onions for 2 minutes.

Add the red pepper and stir-fry for 2 minutes. Return the turkey to the wok with the lemon juice, soy sauce and honey. Stir-fry for 1 to 2 minutes, or until the turkey is piping hot. Serve immediately on a bed of frisée, sprinkled with freshly ground black pepper.

Warm Turkey Salad with Julienned Vegetables

STIR-FRIED CRAB AND PAK CHOI SALAD

IF PREFERRED, THE PAK CHOI CAN BE ADDED TO THE WOK AND
STIR-FRIED FOR 1 TO 2 MINUTES AT THE END OF THE COOKING TIME.
EITHER WAY, THIS DELICATE SALAD IS PERFECT FOR ENTERTAINING.

Serves **4**
Preparation time
  8 to 10 minutes
Cooking time **7 to 9 minutes**

2 Tbsp groundnut oil
2 lemon grass stalks, bruised, outer
  leaves discarded
2 kaffir lime leaves
1 red bird's eye chilli, seeded
  and chopped
1 large carrot, peeled and cut
  into julienne strips

1 large courgette, peeled and cut
  into julienne strips
200-g/7-oz can water chestnuts,
  drained and sliced in half
100 g/4 oz unsalted cashews
350 g/12 oz white crab meat, drained if
  canned and defrosted if frozen
2 Tbsp light soy sauce
2 Tbsp rice wine or dry sherry
200 g/7 oz pak choi, shredded

Heat the wok and add the oil. When hot, stir-fry the lemon grass, kaffir lime
leaves, chilli, carrot and courgette for 3 minutes.

Add the water chestnuts and cashews to the wok. Stir-fry for 2 to 3 minutes, or until
the nuts are golden.

Add the crab meat to the wok and stir-fry for 1 minute. Add the soy sauce and rice
wine or sherry, heat through for another 1 to 2 minutes and serve on the shredded
pak choi.

SAUTÉED VENISON, ASPARAGUS AND CHANTERELLE SALAD

IF CHANTERELLE MUSHROOMS ARE UNAVAILABLE, USE OYSTER OR CHESTNUT MUSHROOMS. SLICE THE MUSHROOMS IF THEY ARE LARGE. BEEF FILLET STEAKS CAN REPLACE THE VENISON.

Trim the steak, cut into thin strips and place in a shallow dish. Blend 2 tablespoons of the oil with the vinegar, soy sauce and red currant jelly. Pour over the steak. Cover and leave in the refrigerator for 30 minutes, spooning the marinade over occasionally. Drain, reserving 4 tablespoons of the marinade.

Heat the wok and add the remaining oil. Stir-fry the shallots, garlic and chilli for 1 minute. Add the drained steak and stir-fry for 2 minutes, then remove from the wok with a slotted spoon.

Add the asparagus and mushrooms to the wok and stir-fry for 2 minutes. Return the steak and shallots to the wok with the reserved marinade; stir-fry for 2 to 3 minutes or until the steak is tender.

Add the sliced nectarines to the wok, give a final stir then arrange on top of the radicchio or salad leaves and serve.

Serves **4**
Preparation time **10 minutes plus 30 minutes marinating time**
Cooking time **8 to 10 minutes**

350 g/12 oz venison steaks
3 Tbsp oil
4 Tbsp sherry vinegar
1 Tbsp dark soy sauce
1 Tbsp red currant jelly, warmed
4 shallots, peeled and sliced
2 garlic cloves, peeled and crushed
1 red jalapeño chilli, seeded and chopped
175 g/6 oz baby asparagus spears, cut in half
100 g/4 oz chanterelle mushrooms, wiped, sliced in half if large
2 firm but ripe nectarines, pitted and sliced
Radicchio or assorted salad leaves

PHEASANT WITH TART APPLE AND FRESH MINT

IF PHEASANT BREASTS ARE UNAVAILABLE,
USE DUCK BREASTS OR VENISON STEAKS INSTEAD.

Serves **4**
Preparation time **10 minutes plus**
  30 minutes marinating time
Cooking time **7 minutes**

2 to 3 pheasant breasts
  (about 250 g/10 oz in weight)
1 red jalapeño chilli, seeded and sliced
150 ml/¼ pt apple juice
2 Tbsp chopped fresh mint
1 tsp honey, warmed

2 Tbsp dark soy sauce
2 Tbsp sunflower oil
2 celery stalks, trimmed and sliced thin
1 large apple (such as Granny Smith),
  peeled, cored and sliced
225 g/8 oz baby spinach leaves, rinsed

TO GARNISH
Fresh mint leaves and pecans

Pheasant with Tart Apple and Fresh Mint

Cut the pheasant into thin strips, place in a shallow dish and scatter the chilli on top. Blend the apple juice with the chopped mint, honey and soy sauce and pour over the pheasant. Cover and marinate in the refrigerator for at least 30 minutes, turning the strips over occasionally in the marinade.

When ready to cook, drain the pheasant and reserve 2 to 3 tablespoons of the marinade.

Heat the wok until hot and add 1 tablespoon of the oil. When hot, stir-fry the drained strips for 2 minutes. Remove from the wok and set aside.

Add the remaining oil to the wok and stir-fry the celery for 1 to 2 minutes. Add the apple and return the strips to the wok. Stir-fry for 2 minutes.

Add the reserved marinade to the wok with the spinach. Stir-fry for 1 minute or until the strips are tender. Sprinkle with the mint leaves and pecans and serve.

LEEK, PEPPER AND TOFU SALAD

IT IS IMPORTANT WHEN USING TOFU THAT YOU DRAIN IT FIRST. OTHERWISE IT WILL BE VERY DIFFICULT TO STIR-FRY. TAKE CARE NOT TO OVERCOOK IT.

Serves **4**
Preparation time **10 minutes**
Cooking time **10 to 11 minutes**

2 leeks, trimmed and sliced
250 g/9 oz tofu (bean curd)
2 Tbsp groundnut oil
1 fennel head, trimmed and thinly sliced
1 red pepper, seeded and cut into half-moon slices
1 orange pepper, seeded and cut into half-moon slices

100 g/4 oz sugar snap peas, halved
2 Tbsp hoisin sauce
2 Tbsp dark soy sauce
2 Tbsp rice wine or dry sherry
1 Tbsp hot chilli sauce
1 tsp honey
1 tsp sesame oil
100 g/4 oz pak choi, shredded
100 g/4 oz bean sprouts

Cover the leeks in boiling water and let stand for 4 minutes. Drain and set aside.

Drain the tofu and cut into bite-size cubes. Heat the wok and add 1 tablespoon of the oil. Stir-fry the tofu for 2 to 3 minutes, or until golden. Remove, drain on paper towels, and set aside.

Add the remaining oil to the wok. Stir-fry the fennel, drained leeks, and peppers for 4 minutes. Add the sugar snap peas and tofu and continue to stir-fry for 2 minutes.

Blend the hoisin, soy sauce, rice wine or sherry, hot chilli sauce and honey, and pour into the wok. Continue to stir-fry for 2 minutes. Add the sesame oil and give a final stir to heat through.

Mix the pak choi and bean sprouts together, spoon over the tofu and vegetable stir-fry, and serve.

TROUT, SPINACH AND RASPBERRY SALAD

THIS STUNNING SALAD IS IDEAL TO SERVE ON WARM SUNNY DAYS OR BALMY EVENINGS WHEN YOU ARE EATING *AL FRESCO*. SERVE WITH PLENTY OF CHILLED CHARDONNAY, WARM CRUSTY BREAD AND A MIXED PEPPER SALAD.

Remove the stalks from the parsley, rinse and pat dry with paper towels. Heat 4 tablespoons of the oil in the wok and fry the parsley in small batches for 30 seconds, or until dark green and crisp. Remove and drain on paper towels.

Wipe the wok clean. Remove as many of the fine bones from the trout fillets as possible and cut into 2.5 cm/1 in strips. (Keep the skin on as this keeps the fish together during cooking.)

Heat the wok and add the oil. When hot, add the trout with the chillies and 1 tablespoon of the lime zest and stir-fry for 2 minutes.

Add the spring onions and spinach and stir-fry for 1 minute. Add the vinegar with the pine nuts and continue to stir-fry for 2 minutes, or until the spinach has wilted slightly. Stir in the raspberries and serve immediately, sprinkled with the remaining lime zest and the parsley.

Serves **4**
Preparation time **5 minutes**
Cooking time **6 minutes**

15 g/½ oz curly parsley
5 Tbsp oil
450 g/1 lb trout fillets
½ to 1 tsp dried crushed chillies

2 Tbsp grated lime zest
8 spring onions, trimmed and
   diagonally sliced
225 g/8 oz baby spinach leaves
1 Tbsp raspberry vinegar or
   balsamic vinegar
2 Tbsp toasted pine nuts
100 g/4 oz fresh raspberries

WARM PORK AND MINT SALAD

IT IS IMPORTANT TO BUY GOOD-QUALITY PORK, AND TO CUT IT INTO THIN STRIPS BEFORE MARINATING, TO ENSURE IT IS BEAUTIFULLY TENDER AFTER COOKING.

Serves **4**
Preparation time **10 minutes**
  plus 30 minutes marinating
  time
Cooking time **11 minutes**

350 g/12 oz pork fillet
2 Tbsp red chilli paste (see page 12)
2 Tbsp groundnut oil
1 red onion, peeled and thinly sliced

1 Tbsp lime juice
1 Tbsp light soy sauce
1 to 2 tsp Thai fish sauce (nam pla)
100 g/4 oz cherry tomatoes
2 red eating apples, cored and sliced
2 Tbsp fresh mint leaves
1 tsp sesame oil

TO SERVE
Bitter salad greens

Cut the pork into thin strips and toss it in the red chilli paste. Marinate in the refrigerator for 30 minutes.

Heat the wok and add 1 tablespoon of the oil. Stir-fry the onion for 2 minutes. Remove from the wok and set aside.

Add the remaining oil to the wok and stir-fry the pork for 2 minutes or until sealed. Return the onion to the wok together with the lime juice and soy and fish sauces and continue to stir-fry for 5 minutes.

Add the cherry tomatoes and sliced apple and stir-fry for another 2 minutes. Add the mint and the sesame oil, give a final stir then serve on a bed of bitter salad greens.

WARM GADO GADO SALAD

GADO GADO SALADS CAN BE FOUND THROUGHOUT INDONESIA. EVERY VERSION IS DIFFERENT.

Serves **4**
Preparation time **12 minutes**
Cooking time **9 to 10 minutes**

225 g/8 oz tofu (bean curd), drained
4 Tbsp groundnut oil
1 red onion, peeled and thinly sliced
1 to 2 bird's eye chillies, seeded and finely chopped
½ cucumber, cut into thin strips

100 g/4 oz green beans, trimmed
175 g/6 oz pak choi, shredded
4 Tbsp crunchy peanut butter
4 Tbsp coconut milk or low-fat, plain yoghurt
2 Tbsp roasted peanuts

TO GARNISH
2 medium eggs, hard-boiled, shelled and sliced

Pat the tofu dry with paper towels and cut into small cubes. Heat the wok, add 2 tablespoons of the oil, and fry the tofu for 2 to 3 minutes, or until sealed and lightly golden. Remove from the wok and set aside.

Add the remaining oil to the wok and stir-fry the onion and chillies for 2 minutes. Add the cucumber, green beans and shredded pak choi and stir-fry for 3 minutes. Blend the peanut butter, 4 tablespoons hot water and the coconut milk or yoghurt together until smooth. Add to the wok with the tofu. Continue to cook for 2 minutes, or until the vegetables are done but still crisp. Sprinkle with the peanuts, garnish with the sliced egg and serve.

WARM SALMON SALAD

SALMON AND CUCUMBER GO WELL TOGETHER, AND THE ADDITION OF THE FRESH MANGO
GIVES THIS SALAD A DELICIOUS NEW TWIST.

Peel the cucumber, cut in half then scoop out and discard the seeds. Slice thin and place in a colander, sprinkling with a little salt. Let stand for 20 minutes, rinse thoroughly in cold water and set aside.

Heat the wok and add 1 tablespoon of oil. Stir-fry the chillies for 1 minute, remove from the wok and drain on paper towels. Set aside. Cut the salmon into thin strips.

Reheat the wok and add the remaining oil. When hot, stir-fry the mushrooms and pepper for 3 minutes. Add the salmon and mango and continue to stir-fry for 2 minutes, or until the salmon is tender.

Stir in the fish, soy and plum sauces. Add the spring onions, the cucumber and the peanuts. Continue to stir for 1 minute, or until hot. Serve on the spinach leaves, sprinkled with the chopped coriander and chillies.

Serves **4**
Preparation time **10 minutes**
   plus 20 minutes standing time
Cooking time **7 minutes**

1 large cucumber
1 to 2 Tbsp salt
2 Tbsp groundnut oil
2 to 3 red serrano chiles, seeded
   and chopped
350 g/12 oz salmon fillets,
   skinned
175 g/6 oz oyster mushrooms,
   wiped and sliced

1 red pepper, seeded
   and chopped
1 mango, peeled, pitted and
   chopped
1 Tbsp Thai fish sauce (nam pla)
2 Tbsp light soy sauce
2 Tbsp plum sauce
8 spring onions, trimmed and
   diagonally sliced
3 Tbsp roasted peanuts
Baby spinach leaves to serve
1 Tbsp chopped fresh coriander

DESSERTS

BRANDIED PINEAPPLE

TO CHECK IF A PINEAPPLE IS RIPE, SIMPLY SMELL IT: IF THERE IS A STRONG PINEAPPLE AROMA AND THE LEAVES
FROM THE PLUME ARE EASILY REMOVED WHEN LIGHTLY PULLED, THE PINEAPPLE IS READY TO EAT.

Serves **4**
Preparation time **7 minutes**
Cooking time **6 minutes**

1 large just-ripe pineapple
25 g/1 oz butter
3 Tbsp orange juice
3 Tbsp caster sugar
4 Tbsp brandy
50 g/2 oz toasted pecans, sliced
Grated orange zest
2 tsp dark brown sugar
Thick Greek yoghurt

Discard the plume and skin and cut the pineapple into thick slices. Remove the centre core and cut the remainder into chunks.

Heat the butter in the wok and add the pineapple chunks. Cook over a high heat for 1 to 2 minutes, or until the pineapple begins to brown.

Add the sugar to the wok with the brandy and stir-fry until the fruit begins to caramelize.

Sprinkle with the nuts, orange zest and brown sugar and serve with spoonfuls of yoghurt.

FRUITS WITH PASSION FRUIT SAUCE

PASSION FRUITS ARE RIPE WHEN THEY ARE REALLY WRINKLED AND LOOK ALMOST PAST THEIR BEST.

Serves **4**
Preparation time **15 minutes**
Cooking time **10 minutes**

FOR THE PASSION FRUIT SAUCE
75 g/3 oz caster sugar
2 Tbsp Cointreau
3 ripe passion fruits

FOR THE FRUITS
50 g/2 oz unsalted butter
1 ripe mango, peeled, pitted
  and cubed
175 g/6 oz strawberries, hulled,
  cut in half if large
100 g/4 oz seedless red grapes
100 g/4 oz seedless green
  grapes

TO SERVE
Waffles or pancakes and
  ice cream

Place the sugar with 150 ml/¼ pt water in the wok and heat gently until the sugar has dissolved. Bring to the boil and boil for 3 minutes. Remove from the heat and stir in the Cointreau. Scoop out the seeds and any juice from the passion fruit and add to the syrup. Set aside until required.

Wipe the wok clean, then add the butter and place over a gentle heat until melted. Add the fruits and gently stir-fry for 3 minutes, or until the fruits are heated through. Add the passion fruit sauce, bring to the boil and serve immediately with ice cream on waffles or pancakes.

TOFFEE APPLES AND BANANAS

THIS DELICIOUS DESSERT IS POPULAR WITH ADULTS AND CHILDREN ALIKE.

Peel, core and cut the apples into thick slices. Slice the bananas and toss both fruits in the lemon juice.

Blend the flours together. Mix in the egg and about 1 teaspoon of the sesame oil to form a very thick batter.

Heat the groundnut oil and the remaining sesame oil in the wok to 190°C/375°F. Dip the apples and bananas into the batter, allowing any excess to drip back into the batter. Fry in small batches for 2 minutes, or until golden. Remove and drain on paper towels. Repeat until all the fruit has been fried.

When ready to serve, fill a mixing bowl with cold water and some ice cubes. Reheat the oil to 180°C/350°F and fry the fruit again, a few at a time, for another 2 minutes. Drain on paper towels.

Place the sugar, sesame seeds and 2 tablespoons of the oil from the deep-frying into a heavy-based pan. Place over a moderate heat until the sugar melts and begins to caramelize. Take care not to burn the sugar.

Once the caramel is light golden, add the fried fruits, a few at a time. Stir the fruits in the caramel until they are coated, then remove and plunge into the ice water for a few seconds until the caramel is hard. Remove. Repeat until all the fruits have been used, then serve.

Serves **6**
Preparation time **15 minutes**
Cooking time **20 minutes**

2 firm eating apples

2 firm bananas

2 Tbsp lemon juice

3 Tbsp plain flour

3 Tbsp cornflour

1 large egg

2 Tbsp sesame oil

300 ml/½ pt groundnut oil

175 g/6 oz sugar

2 Tbsp sesame seeds

WARM TROPICAL FRUITS

TO MAKE SHAVINGS OF FRESH COCONUT, SIMPLY CRACK OPEN A FRESH COCONUT; AFTER DRAINING OFF THE MILK, SHAVE OFF THIN STRIPS WITH A VEGETABLE PEELER. THE SHAVINGS CAN BE DRIED AND STORED IN AN AIRTIGHT JAR FOR LATER USE.

Serves **4**
Preparation time **10 minutes**
Cooking time **7 to 8 minutes**

4 Tbsp honey
1 Tbsp golden syrup
6 star anise
175 g/6 oz fresh lychees,
    peeled and stoned
1 large mango, peeled, pitted
    and diced
1 large papaya, peeled, seeded
    and diced
2 bananas, peeled and sliced

TO GARNISH
Freshly shaved coconut

TO SERVE
Coconut or vanilla ice cream

Place the honey, syrup, star anise, and 1 cup water in the wok and bring to a boil. Boil gently for 3 minutes. Add all the fruit and heat gently for 3 minutes, or until warm.

Serve immediately, decorated with the shaved fresh coconut and scoops of ice cream.

GINGERED PINEAPPLE

THIS DELICIOUS DESSERT IS EASY AND QUICK TO PREPARE AND IS PERFECT TO SERVE FOR ANY OCCASION.

Serves **4**
Preparation time **5 minutes**
Cooking time **7 minutes**

1 large ripe pineapple
50 g/2 oz caster sugar
5 cm/2 in piece root ginger,
    chopped
100 g/4 oz chopped stem ginger
3 Tbsp ginger syrup (from the
    stem ginger jar) or ginger wine
3 fresh figs

TO GARNISH
2 tbsp toasted flaked almonds

Discard the plume, skin and central core from the pineapple and cut into chunks. Set aside.

Place the sugar into the wok with the chopped ginger and 250 ml/8 fl oz water and bring to the boil. Boil gently for 3 minutes then strain off the ginger.

Add the pineapple chunks, the stem ginger and syrup, and simmer gently for 2 minutes. Cut the figs into quarters, add to the wok, and continue to simmer for another 2 minutes, or until heated through.

Serve sprinkled with the toasted almonds.

SUMMER FRUITS WITH
ICED MASCARPONE

THIS DESSERT IS SO SIMPLE TO COOK AND SO DELICIOUS TO EAT. IF TIME IS TIGHT, SIMPLY SERVE THE MASCARPONE IN SPOONFULS WITH THE BERRIES.

Set the freezer to rapid freeze. Beat the cheese with the icing sugar until creamy. Lightly whip the cream until softly peaking then fold into the cream cheese together with the Grand Marnier.

Spoon the mixture into a freezable container and freeze for 1 hour (or use an ice-cream maker and follow the manufacturer's instructions). Remove from the freezer, beat then freeze again for 2 hours. Beat again to break up the ice crystals then return to the freezer for a further 2 hours or until solid. Allow to soften in the refrigerator for 30 minutes before using.

Heat the caster sugar with 150 ml/¼ pt of water in the wok until the sugar has dissolved. Boil gently for 3 minutes then add the vanilla bean or essence and simmer for 2 minutes.

Add the cleaned fruits to the wok and simmer for 3 minutes then serve warm with the iced mascarpone, garnished with mint sprigs.

Serves **4**
Preparation time **10 minutes plus 5 hours freezing time**
Cooking time **8 minutes**

250-g/9-oz tub mascarpone cheese
3 Tbsp icing sugar, sifted
300 ml/½ pt double cream
4 Tbsp Grand Marnier
50 g/2 oz caster sugar
1 vanilla bean or a few drops vanilla essence
450 g/1 lb mixed summer berries, cleaned

TO GARNISH
Mint leaves

INDEX